AUDIO ACCESS INCLUDED
Recorded Accompaniments Online

Young Men's Edition

TEEN BROADWAY
SONGS OF THE 2010s

12 SONGS FROM TEEN MUSICAL THEATRE ROLES

T0084207

PLAYBACK+
Speed • Pitch • Balance • Loop

To access audio visit:
www.halleonard.com/mylibrary

Enter Code
6437-3337-3279-8984

ISBN 978-1-5400-6023-5

Visit Hal Leonard Online at
www.halleonard.com

Contact us:
Hal Leonard
7777 West Bluemound Road
Milwaukee, WI 53213
Email: info@halleonard.com

In Europe, contact:
Hal Leonard Europe Limited
42 Wigmore Street
Marylebone, London, W1U 2RN
Email: info@halleonardeurope.com

In Australia, contact:
Hal Leonard Australia Pty. Ltd.
4 Lentara Court
Cheltenham, Victoria, 3192 Australia
Email: info@halleonard.com.au

HOW TO USE HAL LEONARD ONLINE AUDIO

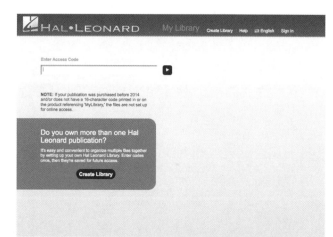

Because of the changing use of media, and the fact that fewer people are using CDs, we have made a shift to companion audio accessible online. In many cases, rather than a book with CD, we now have a book with an access code for online audio, including performances, accompaniments or diction lessons. Each copy of each book has a unique access code. We call this Hal Leonard created system "My Library." It's simple to use.

Go to www.halleonard.com/mylibrary and enter the unique access code found on page one of a relevant book/audio package.

The audio tracks can be streamed or downloaded. If you download the tracks on your computer, you can add the files to a CD or to your digital music library, and use them anywhere without being online. See below for comments about Apple and Android mobile devices.

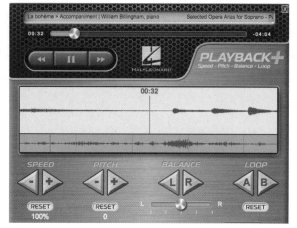

There are some great benefits to the My Library system. **Playback+** is exclusive to Hal Leonard, and when connected to the Internet with this multi-functional audio player you can:

• Change tempo without changing pitch
• Transpose to any key

Optionally, you can create a My Library account, and store all the companion audio you have purchased there. Access your account online at any time, from any device, by logging into your account at www.halleonard.com/mylibrary. Technical help may be found at www.halleonard.com/mylibrary/help/

Apple/iOS

Question: On my iPad and iPhone, the Download links just open another browser tab and play the track. How come this doesn't really download?

Answer: The Safari iOS browser will not allow you to download audio files directly in iTunes or other apps. There are several ways to work around this:

• You can download normally on your desktop computer, saving the files to iTunes. Then, you can sync your iOS device directly to your computer, or sync your iTunes content using an iCloud account.
• There are many third-party apps which allow you to download files from websites into the app's own file manager for easy retrieval and playback.

Android

Files are always downloaded to the same location, which is a folder usually called "Downloads" (this may vary slightly depending on what browser is used (Chrome, Firefox, etc)). Chrome uses a system app called "Downloads" where files can be accessed at any time. Firefox and some other browsers store downloaded files within a "Downloads" folder in the browser itself.

Recently-downloaded files can be accessed from the Notification bar; swiping down will show the downloaded files as a new "card", which you tap on to open. Opening a file depends on what apps are installed on the Android device. Audio files are opened in the device's default audio app. If a file type does not have a default app assigned to it, the Android system alerts the user.

TEEN BROADWAY SONGS OF THE 2010s

CONTENTS

Pianists on the recordings: [1] Brendan Fox, [2] Ruben Piirainen, [3] Richard Walters

The price of this book includes access to recorded accompaniments online,
including **PLAYBACK+**, a multifunctional audio player.
See access information on the title page.

ENJOY THE TRIP
from *Bring It On: The Musical*

Music by Tom Kitt
Lyrics by Amanda Green

Driving mid-tempo Pop (= 83)

RANDALL:

I'm a

stud now, ___ it's clear so it'-ll shock you ___ to hear ___ that

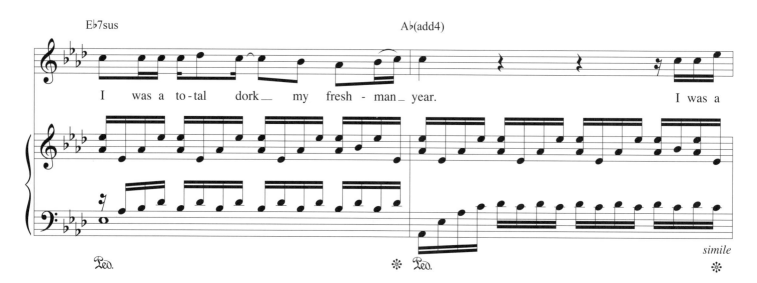

I was a to-tal dork ___ my fresh-man ___ year. I was a

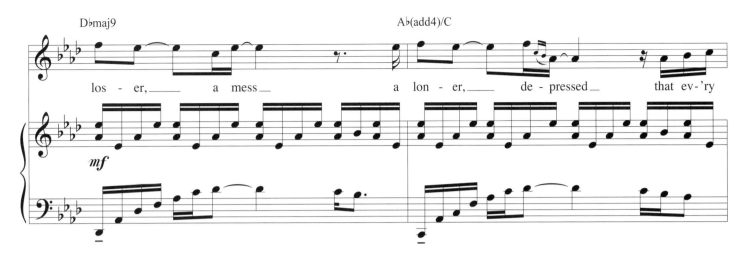

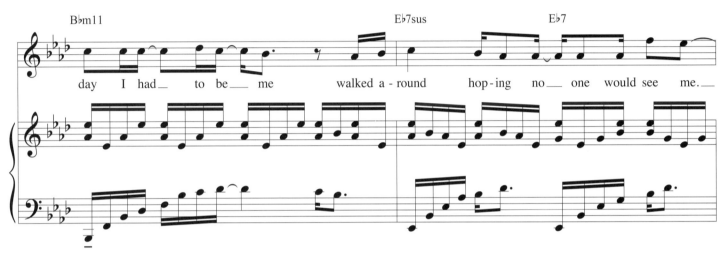

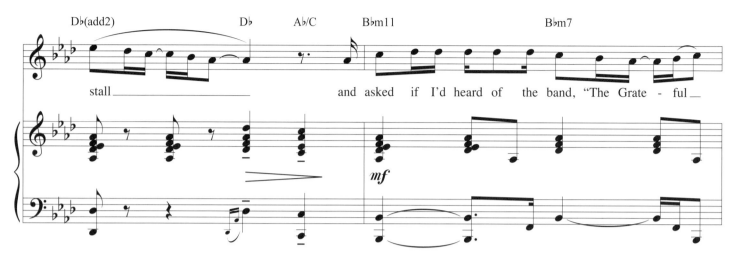

stall _____ and asked if I'd heard of the band, "The Grate - ful __

Dead." And I thought he might __ not be __ quite right __ in the

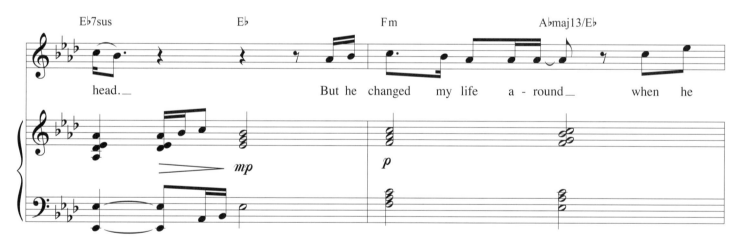

head. __ But he changed my life a - round __ when he

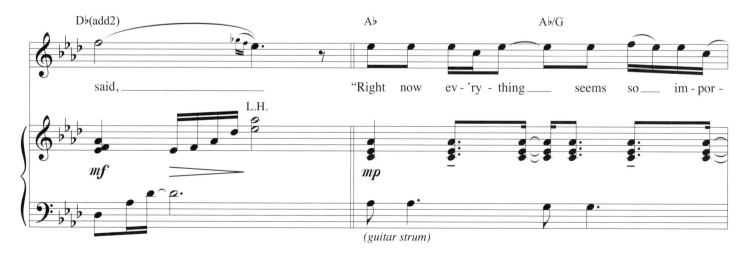

said, _____ "Right now ev - 'ry - thing __ seems so __ im - por -

(guitar strum)

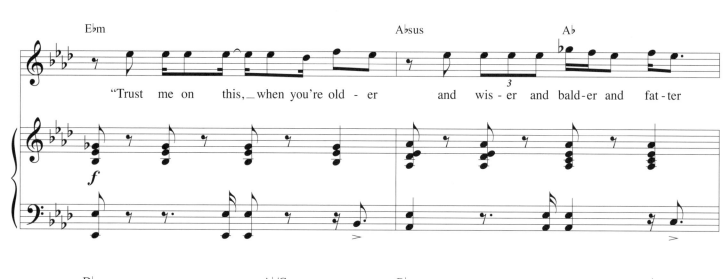

"Trust me on this,_ when you're old - er and wis - er and bald-er and fat - ter

and you look back on this mo - ment in time the on-ly thing that's gon - na mat - ter is did you

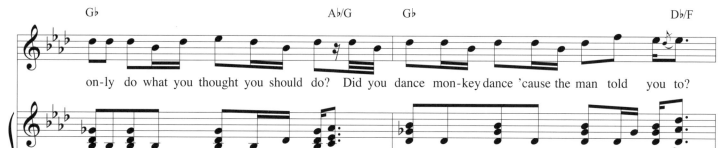

on-ly do what you thought you should do? Did you dance mon-key dance 'cause the man told you to?

Or did you spend your time do - ing what brings joy___ to you?___

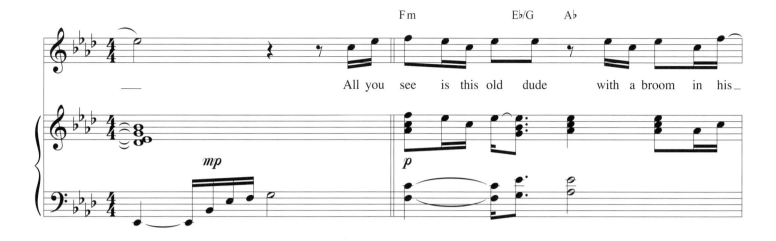

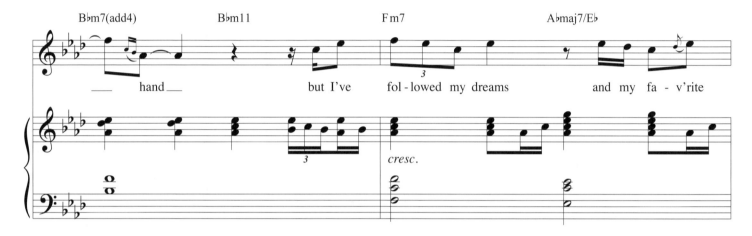

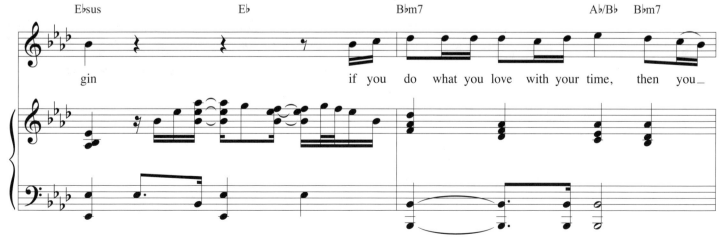

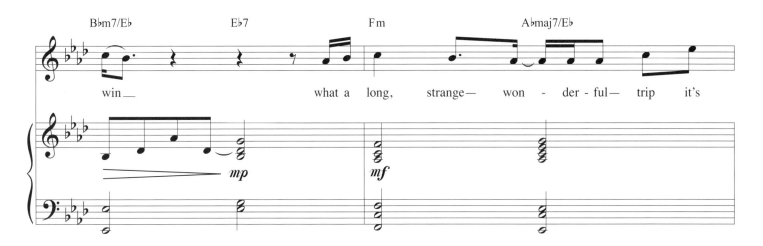

win___ what a long, strange— won - der - ful— trip it's

been!_____ Right now ev - 'ry - thing seems so___ im - por -

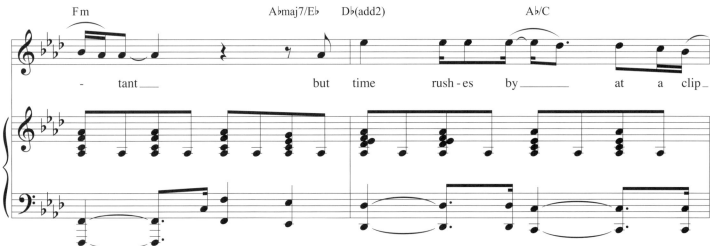

- tant___ but time rush - es by_____ at a clip_

_____ and when you look back, these high_ school years_ will be

GOODBYE
from *Catch Me if You Can*

Lyrics by Scott Wittman and Marc Shaiman
Music by Marc Shaiman

Rock ♩ = 148

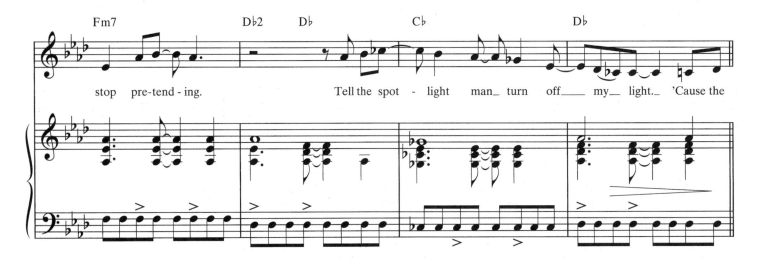

show is done_ now_____ and it's time to leave_ the stage._ Yeah, the

good guy won_ now_____ and the band___ has no_ more songs_

___ to play._ It's a hap - py end - ing, so___ I'll__ say_____ good - bye._

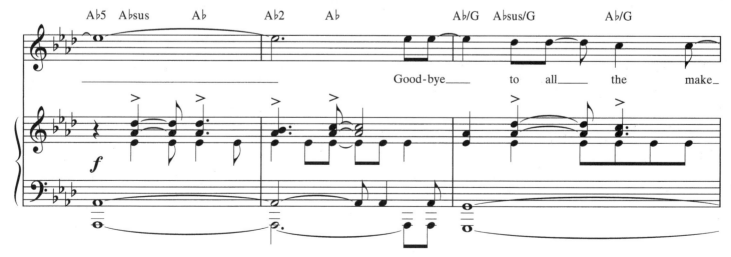

Good-bye___ to all___ the make_

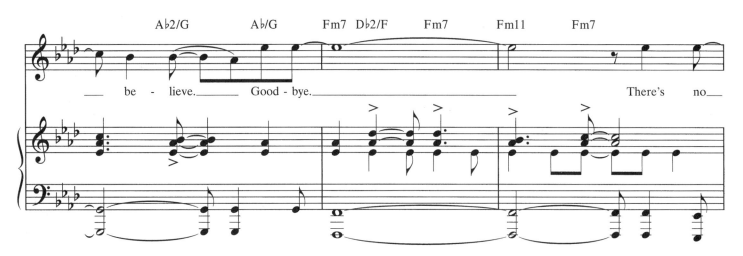

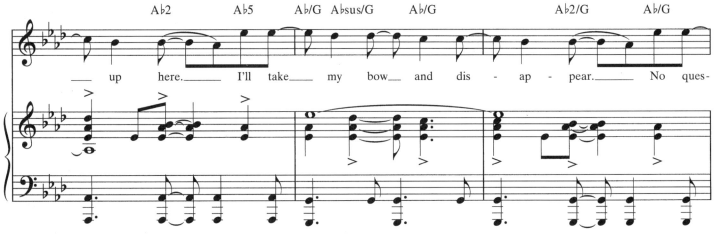

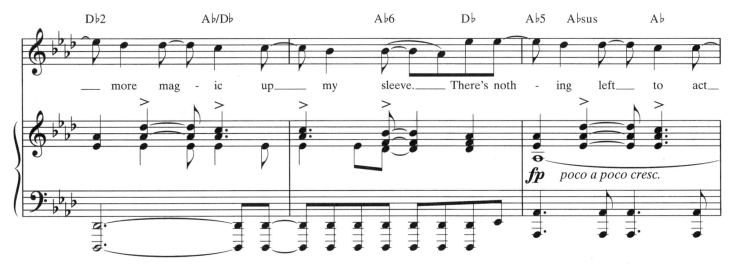

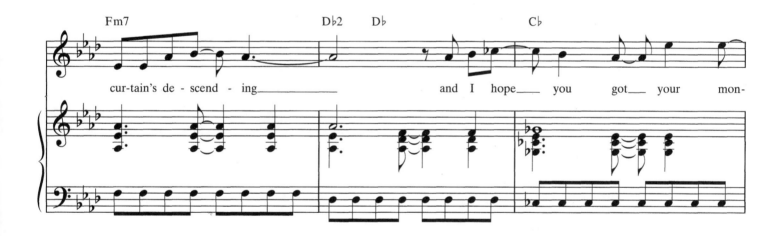

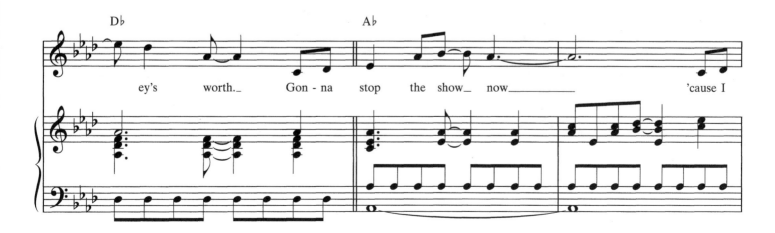

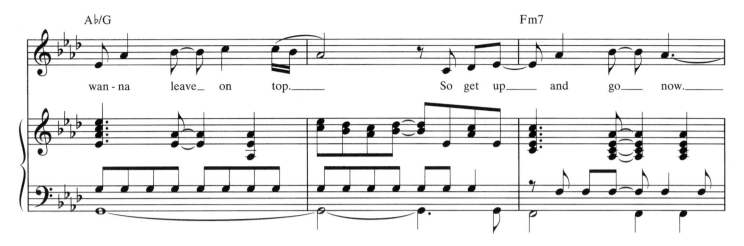

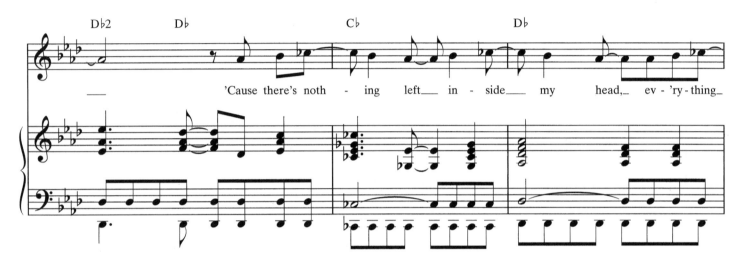

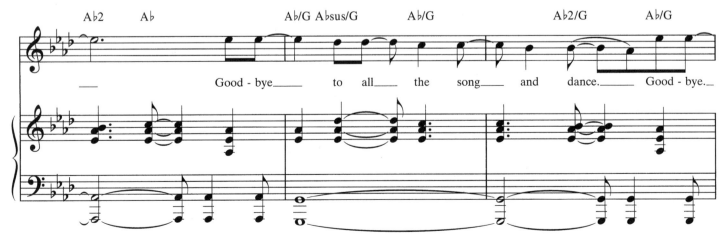

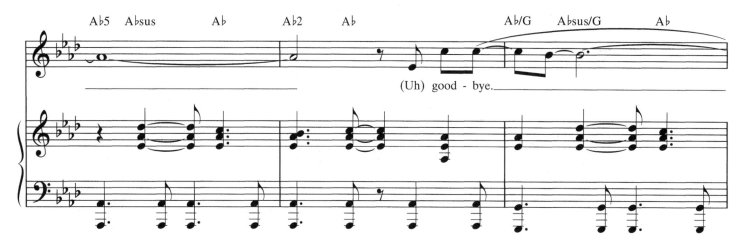

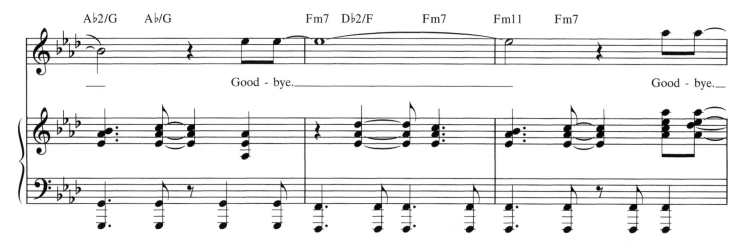

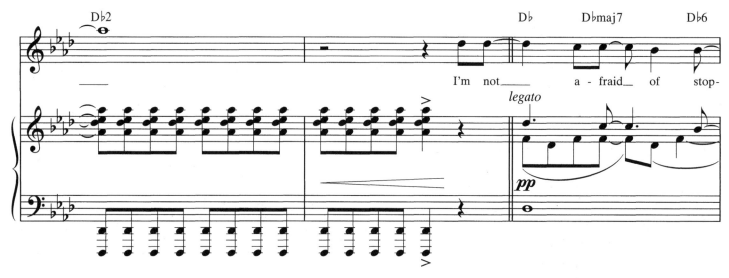

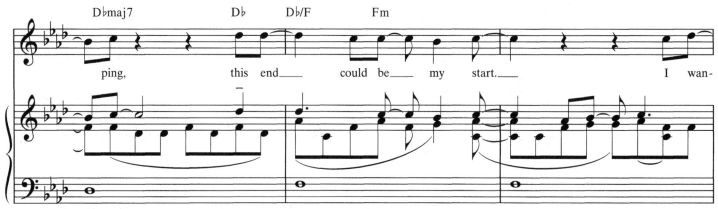

na live__ a life__ and not__ just play__ a part.

I'll walk in - to__ the sun - set, I'll

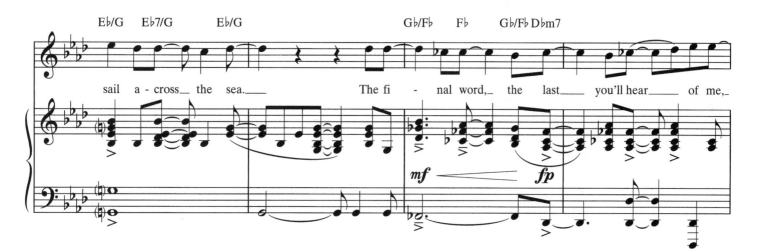

sail a - cross__ the sea.__ The fi - nal word,__ the last__ you'll hear__ of me,__

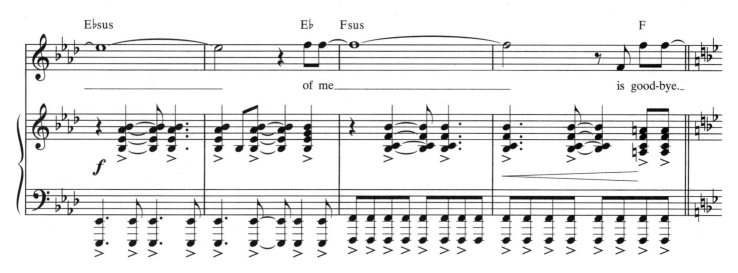

_____ of me_____ is good-bye.__

FOR FOREVER

from *Dear Evan Hansen*

Music and Lyrics by Benj Pasek
and Justin Paul

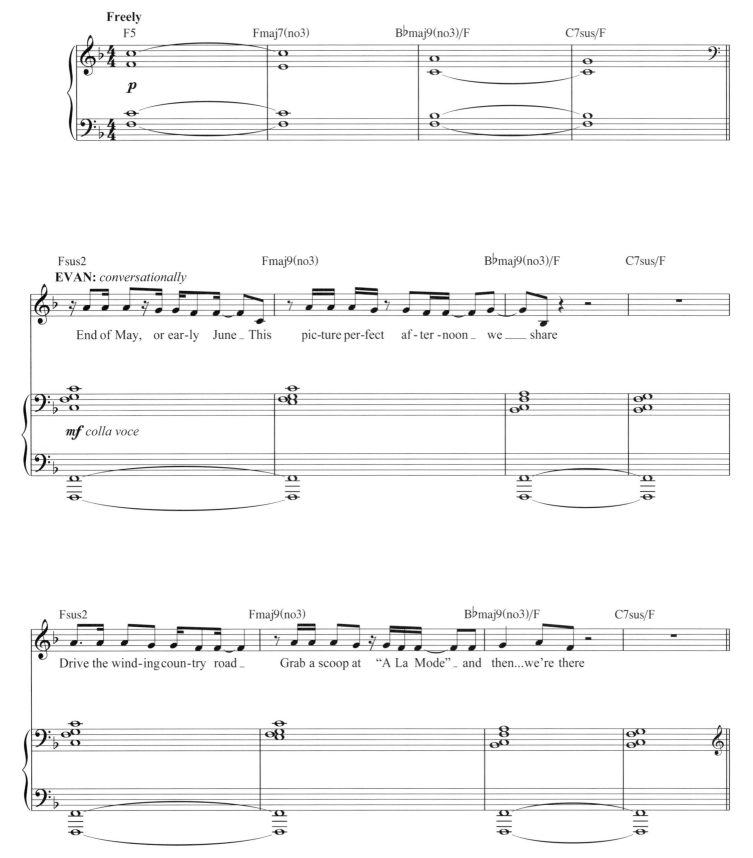

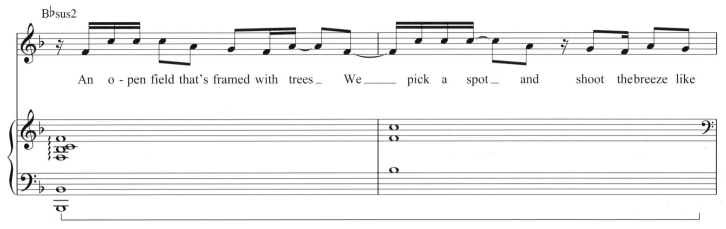

An o-pen field that's framed with trees_ We___ pick a spot_ and shoot thebreeze like

bud-dies do ___ Quot-ing songs_ by our fa-v'rite bands_ Tell-ing jokes_ no one_ un-der-stands_ ex-

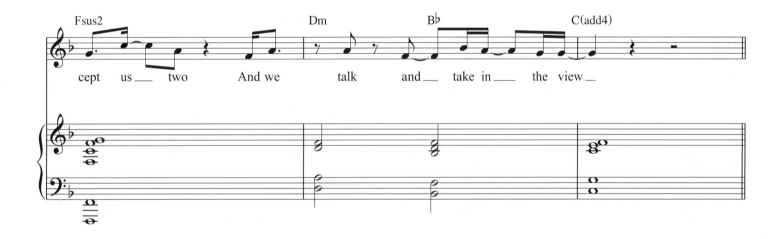

cept us_ two And we talk and_ take in_ the view_

In time (♩ = 91)

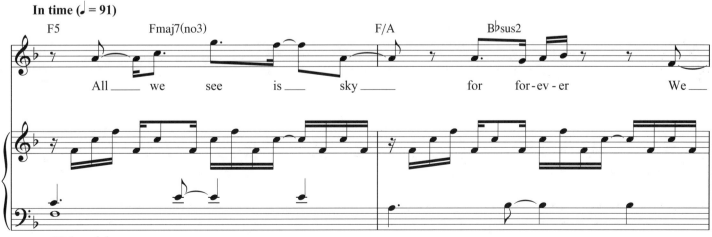

All___ we see is_ sky___ for for-ev-er We___

With pedal

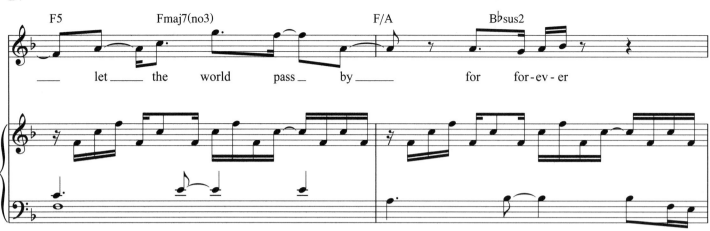

let ___ the world pass ___ by ___ for for-ev-er

Feels ___ like we could ___ go on ___ for for-ev-er this way

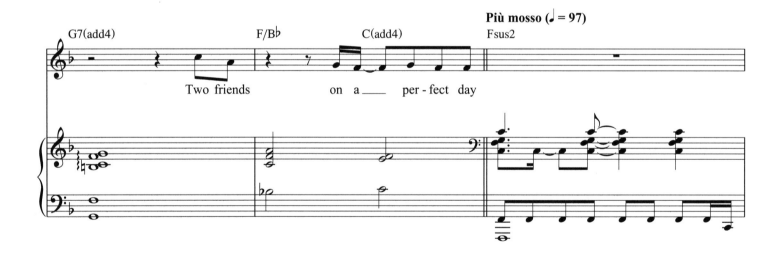

Two friends on a ___ per-fect day

Più mosso ($\quad$ = 97)

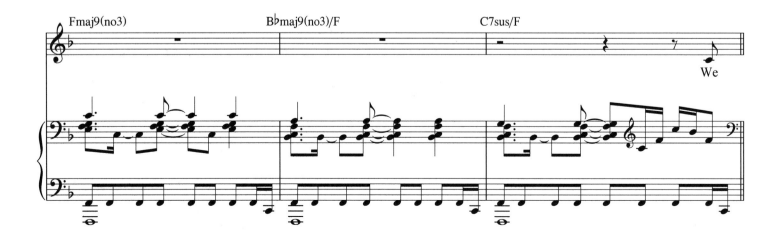

We

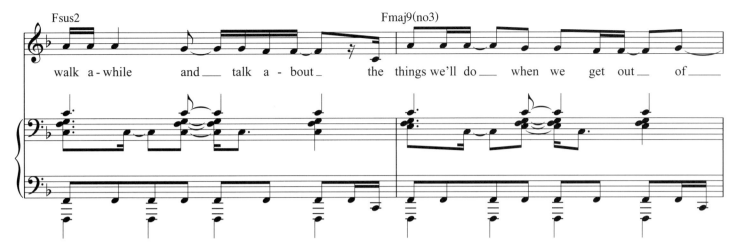

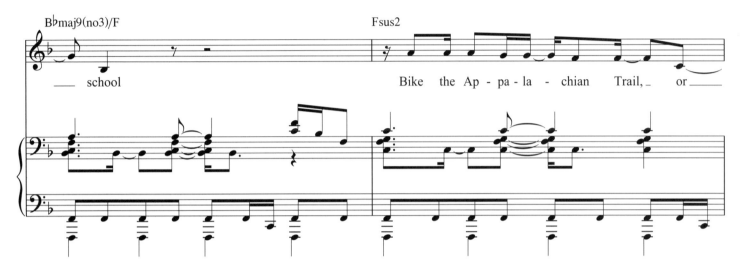

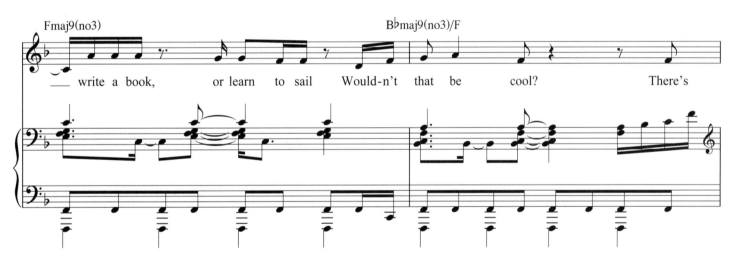

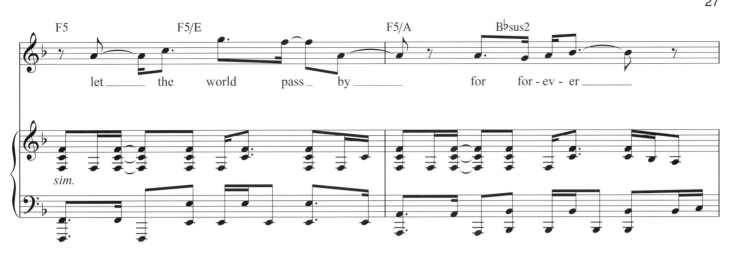

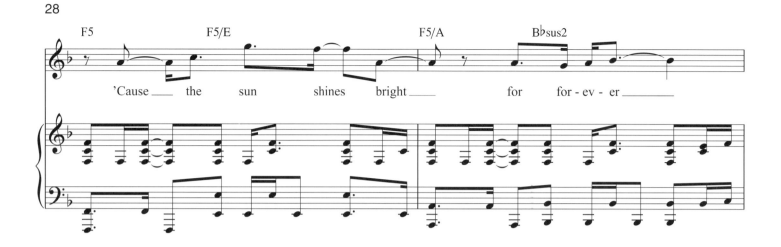

'Cause ___ the sun shines bright ___ for for - ev - er ___

Like ___ we'll be al - right ___ for for - ev - er this way ___

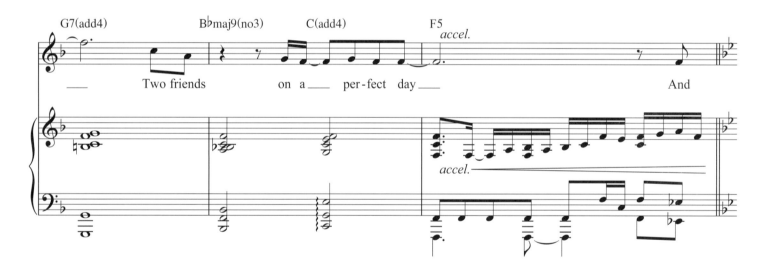

___ Two friends on a ___ per-fect day ___ And

there he goes, ___ rac-in' toward ___ the tall - est tree ___ From

far a-cross__ a yel-low field__ I hear__ him call-in' "Fol-low me!"

There we go__ won-der-in' how the world__ might look__ from up__ so__ high__

Picking up speed (♩ = 100)

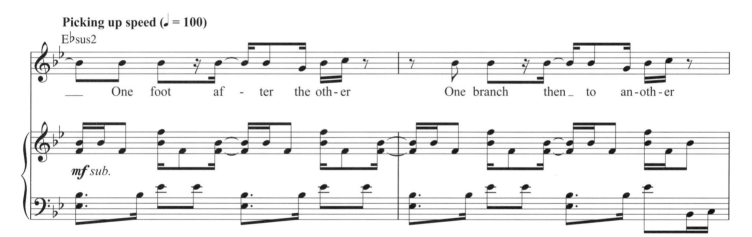

__ One foot af-ter the oth-er One branch then__ to an-oth-er

I climb high - er and high-er I climb 'til__ the en-tire__

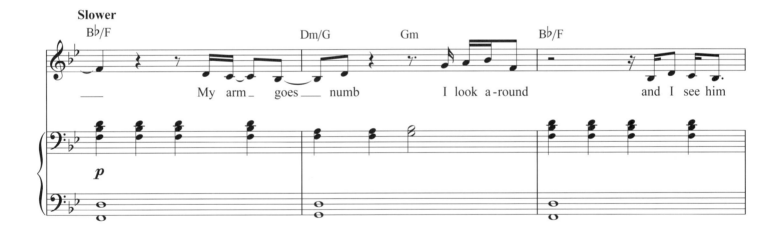

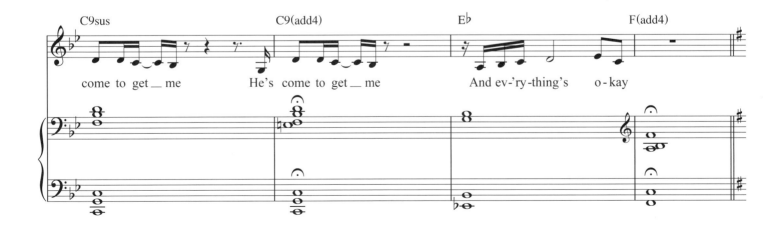

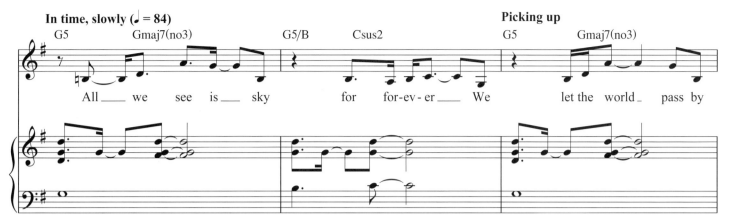

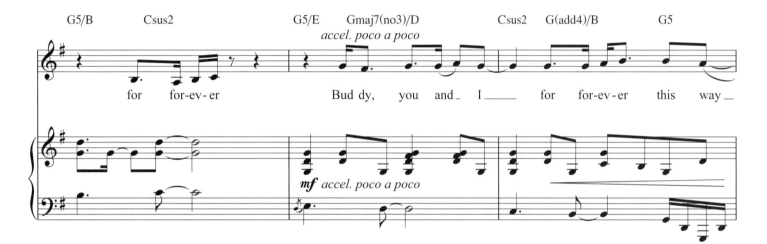

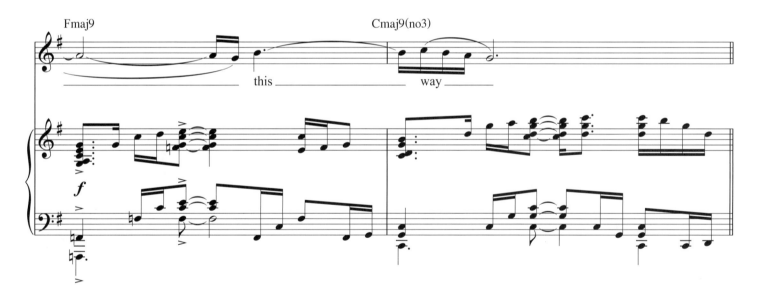

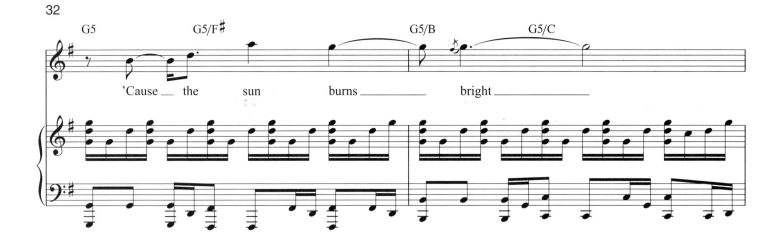

’Cause ___ the sun burns _____ bright _____

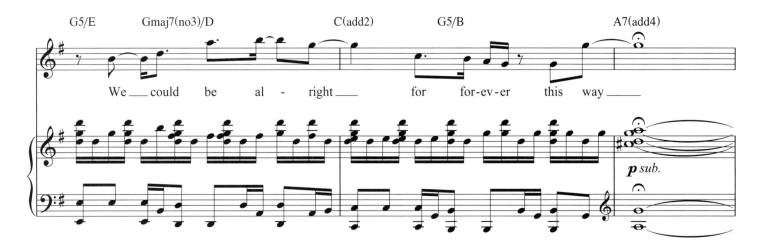

We ___ could be al - right ___ for for-ev-er this way _____

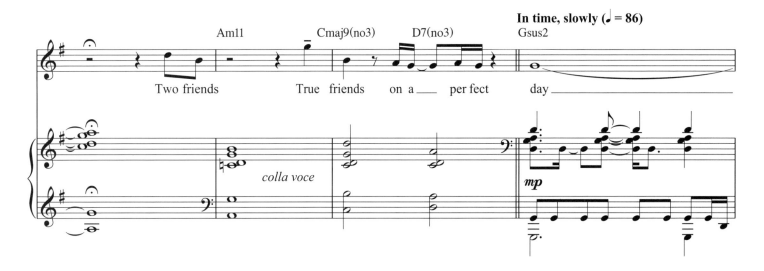

Two friends   True friends   on a ___ per fect   day _____

In time, slowly (♩ = 86)

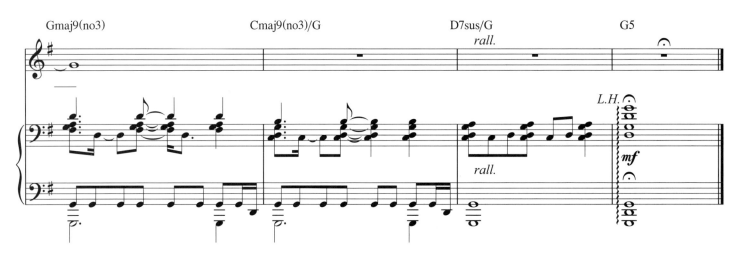

I BELIEVE
from the Broadway Musical *The Book of Mormon*

Words and Music by Trey Parker,
Robert Lopez and Matt Stone

Chorus parts have been omitted from this solo voice edition.

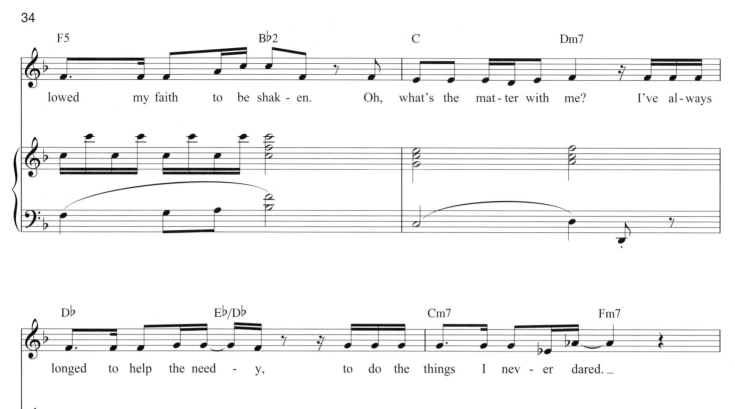

lowed my faith to be shak - en. Oh, what's the mat - ter with me? I've al - ways

longed to help the need - y, to do the things I nev - er dared. _

This was the time for me to step up, so then why was I so scared? A

Più mosso (colla voce)

war - lord who shoots peo - ple in the face. What's so scar - y a - bout that? I must

Broadly

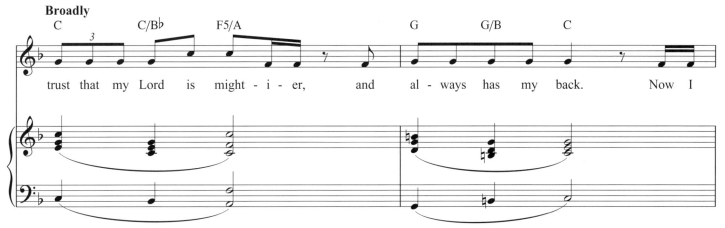

trust that my Lord is might - i - er, and al - ways has my back. Now I

Steady pop, in 4 (♩ = 82)

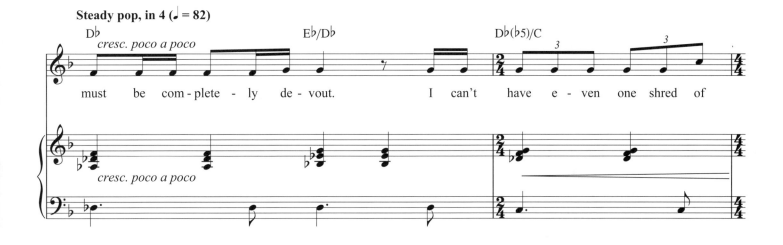

must be com - plete - ly de - vout. I can't have e - ven one shred of

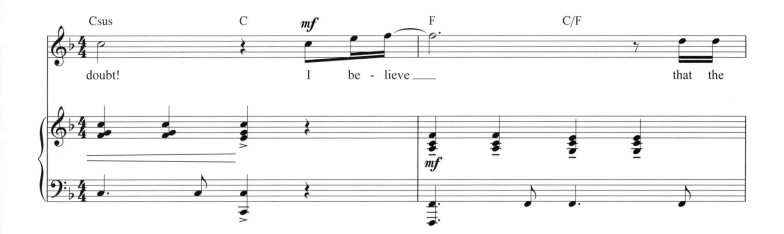

doubt! I be - lieve ___ that the

Lord God cre - at - ed the u - ni - verse. I be - lieve ___ that he sent his on - ly Son to die ___

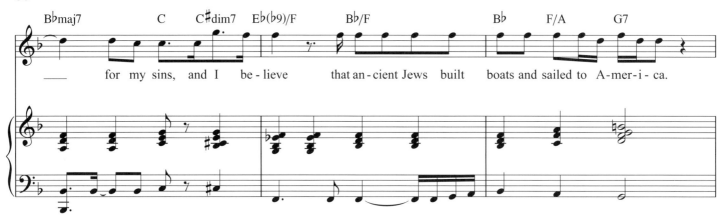

for my sins, and I be - lieve that an - cient Jews built boats and sailed to A - mer - i - ca.

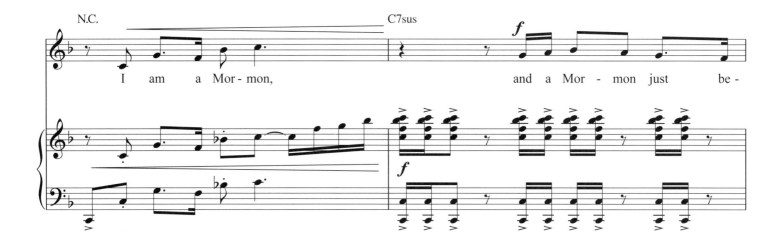

I am a Mor - mon, and a Mor - mon just be -

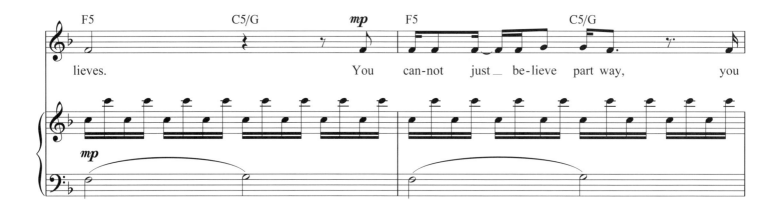

lieves. You can - not just__ be - lieve part way, you

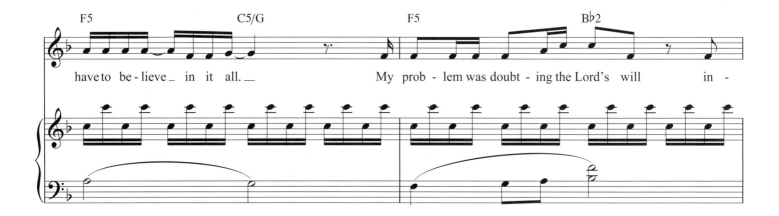

have to be - lieve__ in it all.__ My prob - lem was doubt - ing the Lord's will in -

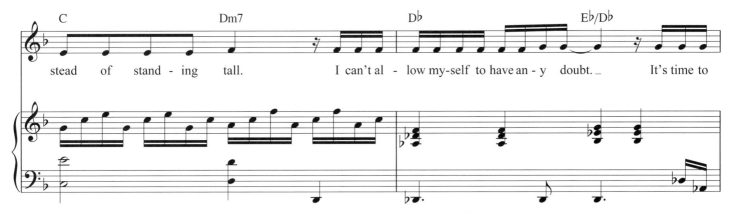

stead of stand - ing tall. I can't al - low my-self to have an - y doubt. _ It's time to

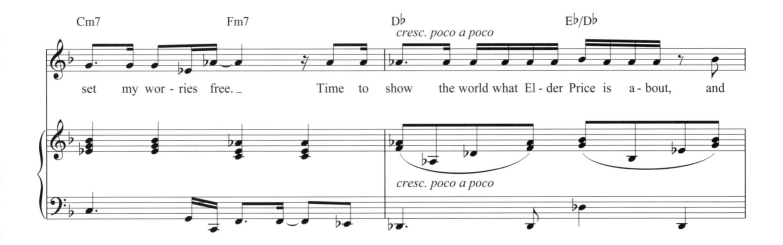

cresc. poco a poco

set my wor - ries free. _ Time to show the world what El - der Price is a - bout, and

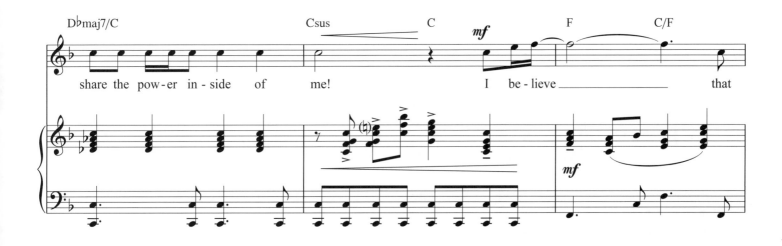

share the pow - er in - side of me! I be - lieve _____ that

God has a plan for all __ of us. I be - lieve __ that plan in - volves

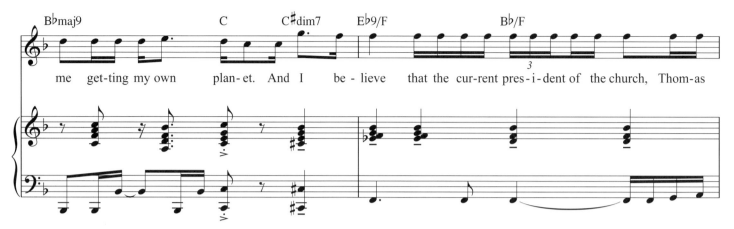

me get-ting my own plan-et. And I be-lieve that the cur-rent pres-i-dent of the church, Thom-as

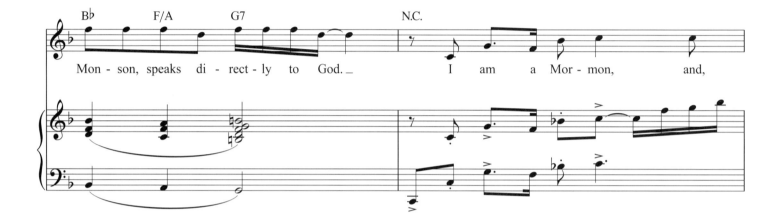

Mon - son, speaks di - rect - ly to God. _ I am a Mor - mon, and,

dang it, a Mor - mon just be - lieves. I

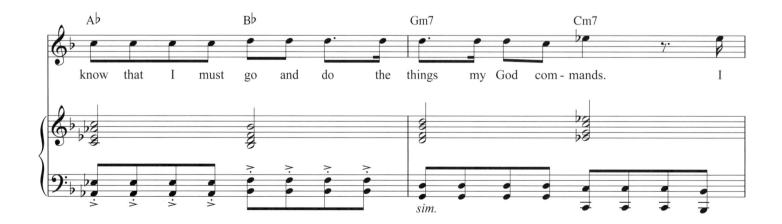

know that I must go and do the things my God com - mands. I

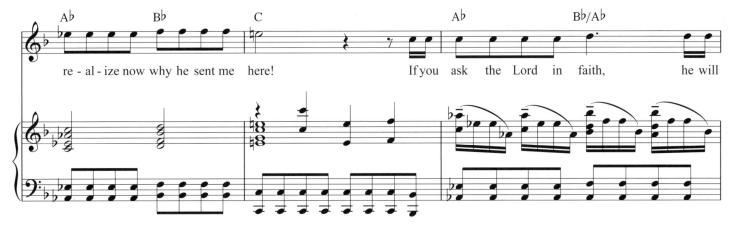

re - al - ize now why he sent me here! If you ask the Lord in faith, he will

al - ways an - swer you. Just be - lieve in him and have no fear.

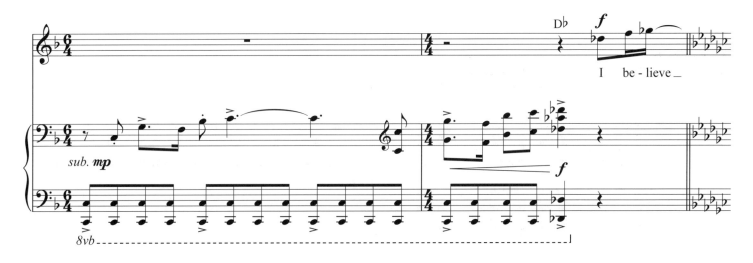

I be - lieve _

_____ that Sa - tan has a hold _ of you. I be - lieve _ that the Lord

feel so in-cred-i-ble to be shar-ing my faith_ with you. The

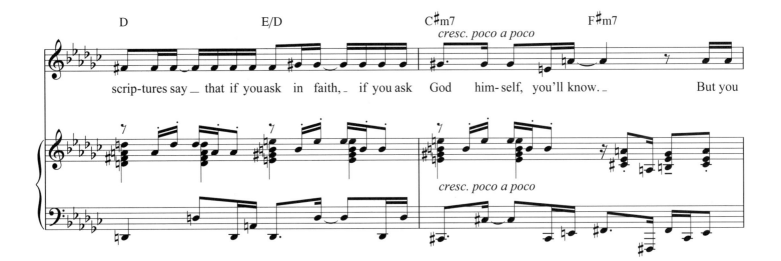

scrip-tures say _ that if you ask in faith, _ if you ask God him-self, you'll know. _ But you

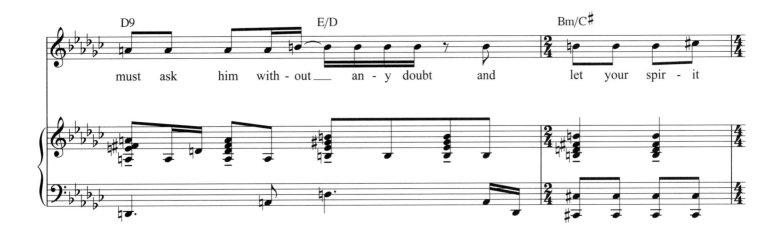

must ask him with-out _ an-y doubt and let your spir-it

grow. I be-lieve _____ that

God lives on a plan-et called Ko-lob. I be-lieve ___ that Je - sus has

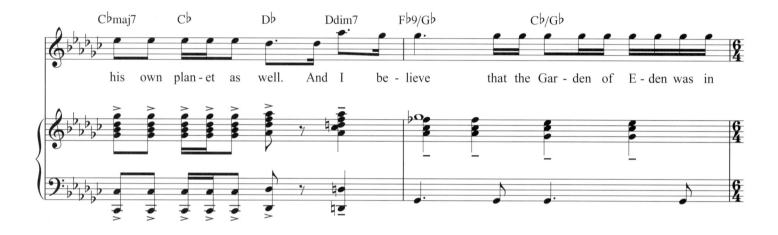

his own plan-et as well. And I be-lieve that the Gar - den of E - den was in

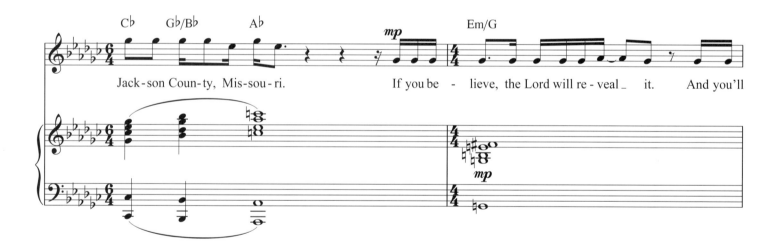

Jack-son Coun-ty, Mis-sou-ri. If you be - lieve, the Lord will re - veal ___ it. And you'll

know it's all true, ___ you'll just feel it. You'll be a Mor - mon, and,

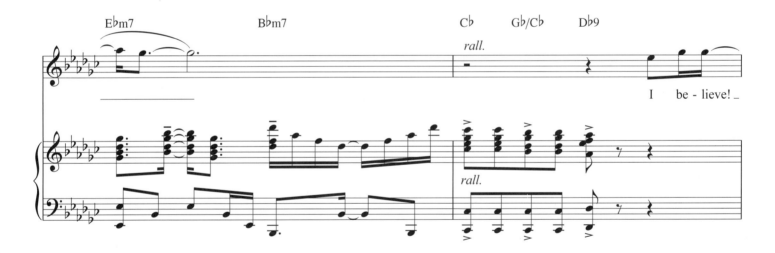

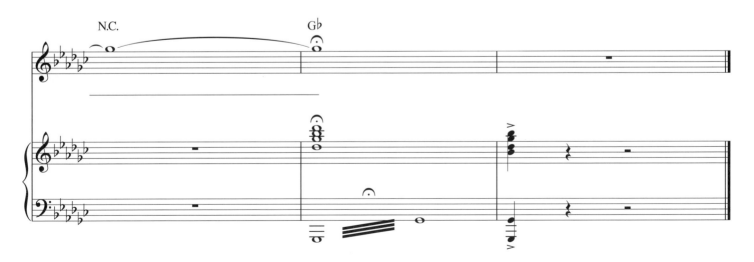

I NEVER PLANNED ON YOU

from *Newsies The Musical*

Music by Alan Menken
Lyrics by Jack Feldman

This has been adapted as a solo, eliminating "Don't Come A-Knocking."

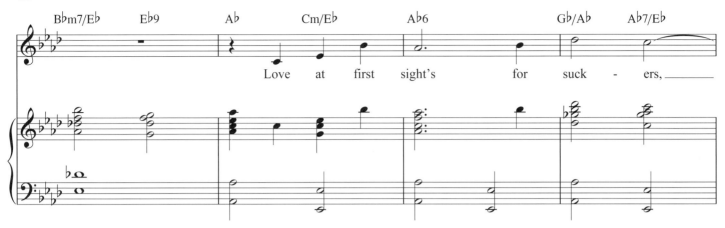

Love at first sight's for suck - ers,

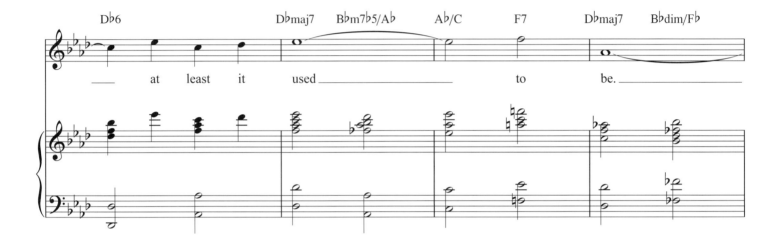

____ at least it used ____ to be. ____

____ No, I nev - er planned on

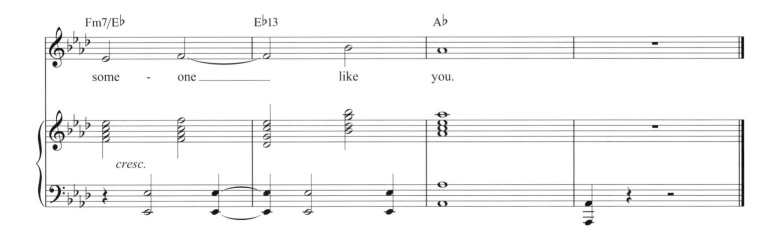

some - one ____ like you.

MY PETERSBURG

from *Anastasia*

Lyrics by Lynn Ahrens
Music by Stephen Flaherty

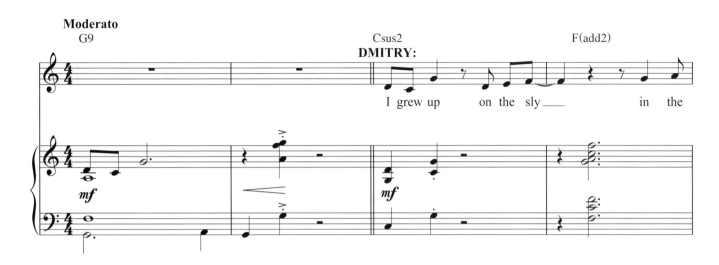

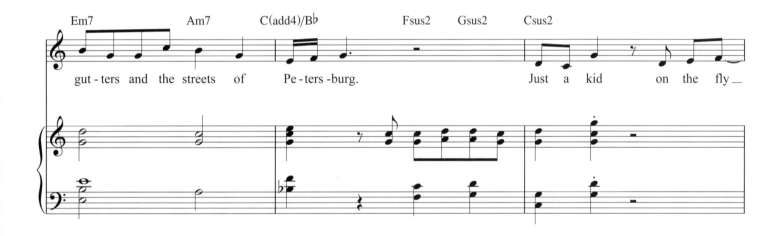

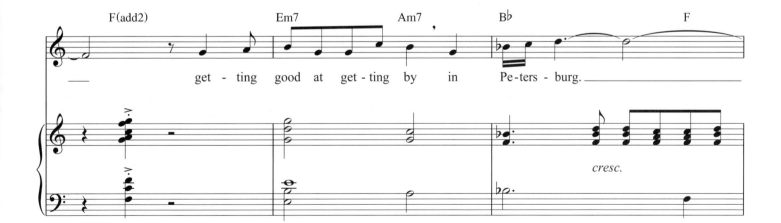

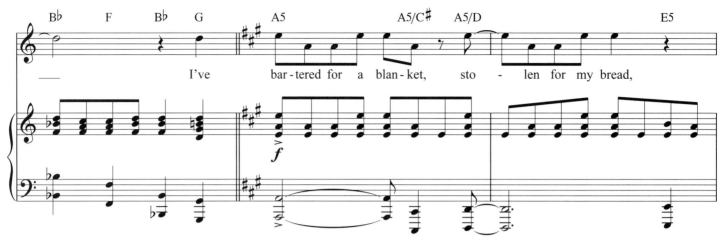

I've bar-tered for a blan-ket, sto - len for my bread,

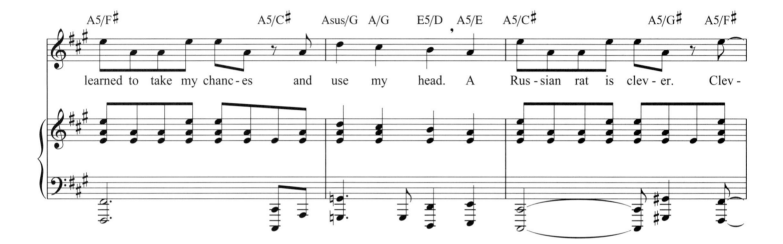

learned to take my chanc-es and use my head. A Rus-sian rat is clev-er. Clev-

- er or he ends up dead! Boils down to:

there are some who sur-vive. Some who don't. Some give up. Some give in.

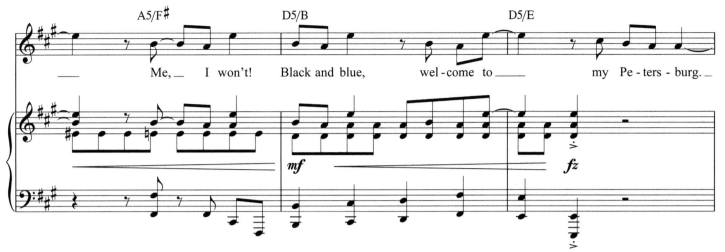

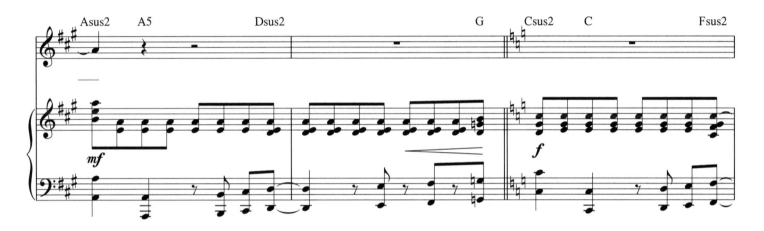

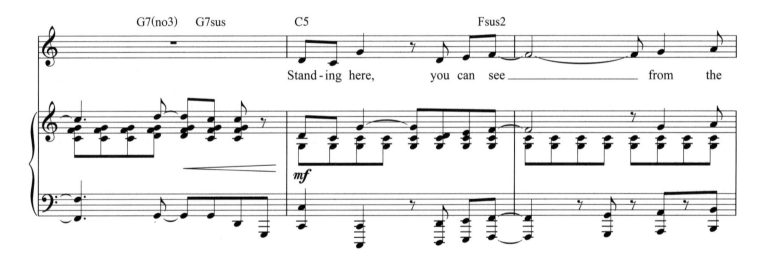

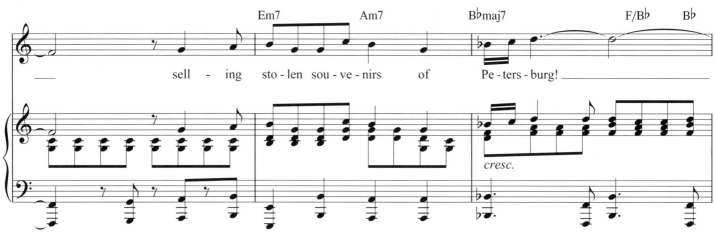

sell - ing sto - len sou - ve - nirs of Pe - ters - burg!

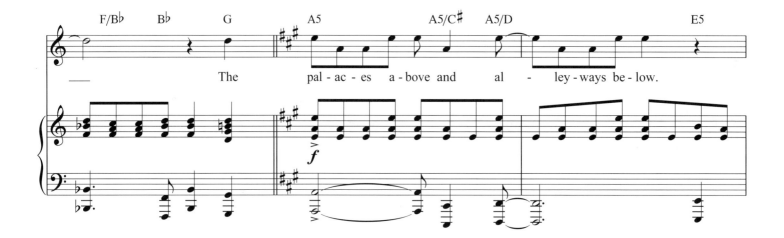

The pal - ac - es a - bove and al - ley - ways be - low.

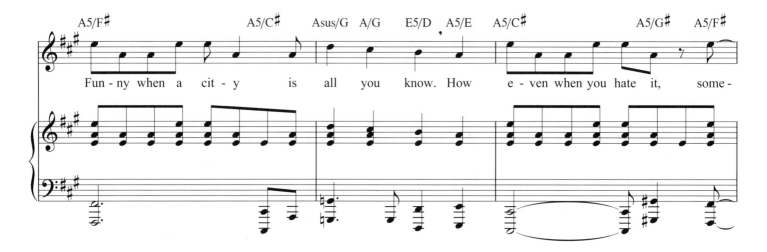

Fun - ny when a cit - y is all you know. How e - ven when you hate it, some -

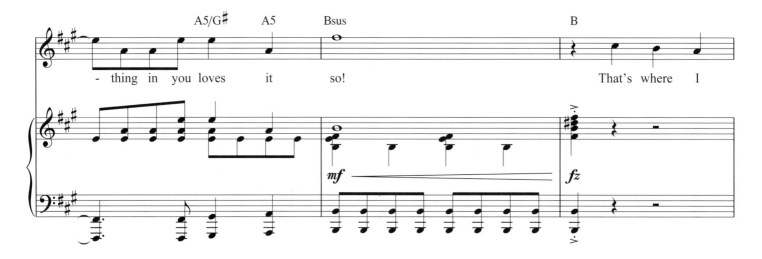

- thing in you loves it so! That's where I

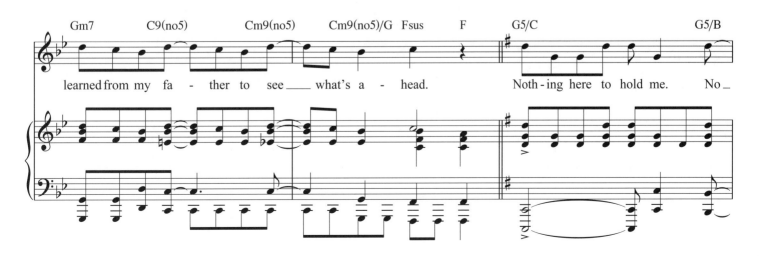

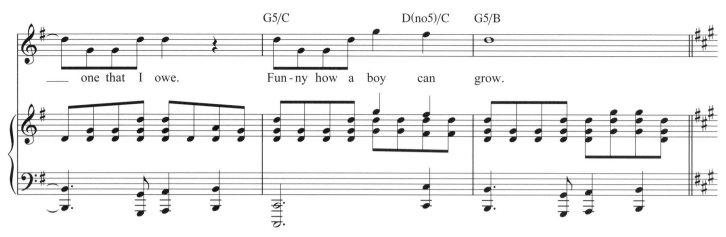

one that I owe. Fun-ny how a boy can grow.

Fun-ny how a cit-y tells __ you when it's time to go!

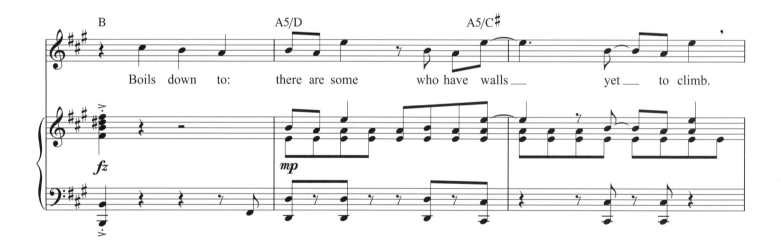

Boils down to: there are some who have walls __ yet __ to climb.

You and I, __ on the fly, __ just __ in time!

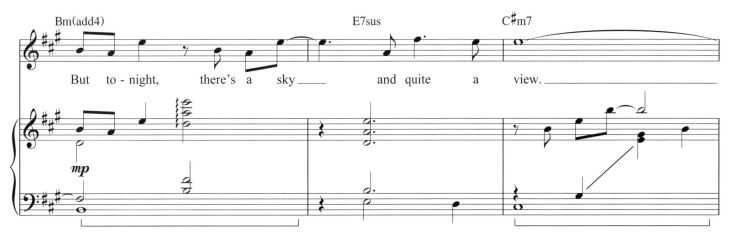

But to-night, there's a sky ___ and quite a view. ___

Wel-come to ___

my Pe - ters - burg. ___

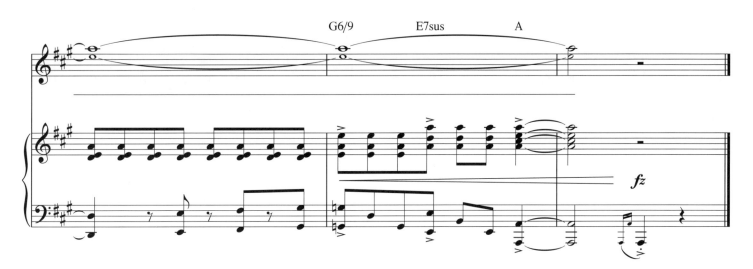

LOSER GEEK WHATEVER

from *Be More Chill*

Words and Music by
Joe Iconis

Gm7   Gm7/Bb   **Rit.** C

was do - ing some-thing that   I nev - er thought that I could

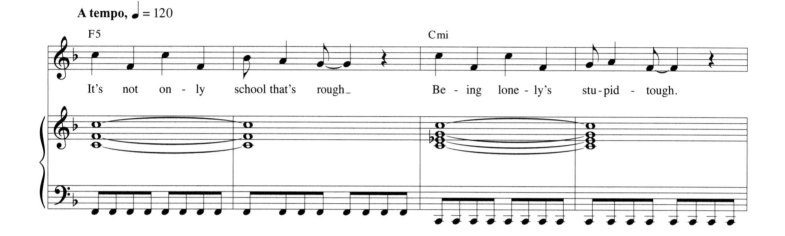

A tempo, ♩ = 120

F5   Cmi

It's   not   on - ly   school that's   rough   Be - ing lone - ly's   stu - pid - tough.

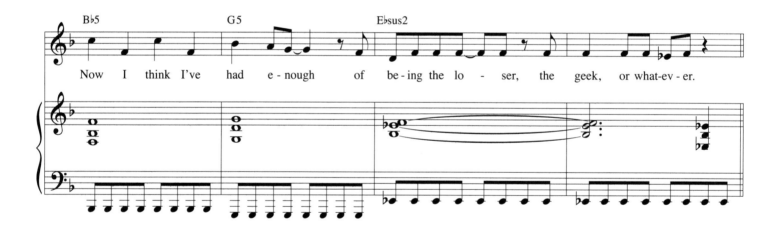

Bb5   G5   Ebsus2

Now I think I've had e - nough   of be - ing the lo - ser,   the   geek,   or what-ev - er.

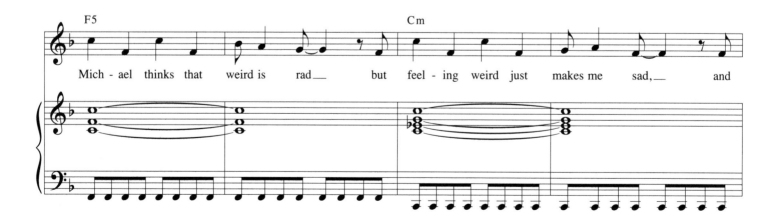

F5   Cm

Mich - ael thinks that weird is rad   but feel - ing weird just makes me sad,   and

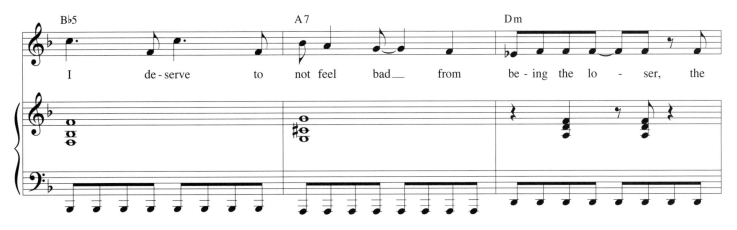

I de-serve to not feel bad___ from be-ing the lo - ser, the

geek, or what-ev - er. Sick of be-ing the lo - ser, the geek, or what-ev - er, yeah!

Woah_____ Uh - huh Uh - huh Uh - huh Woah_____ Uh-huh Uh-huh

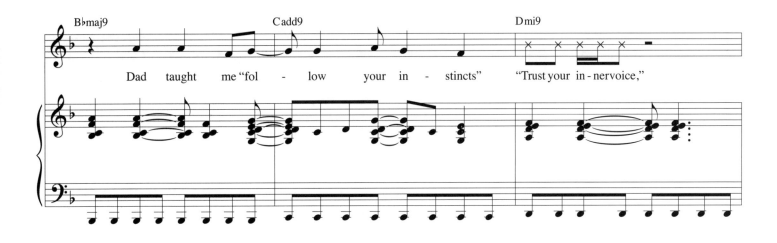

Dad taught me "fol - low your in - stincts" "Trust your in - nervoice,"

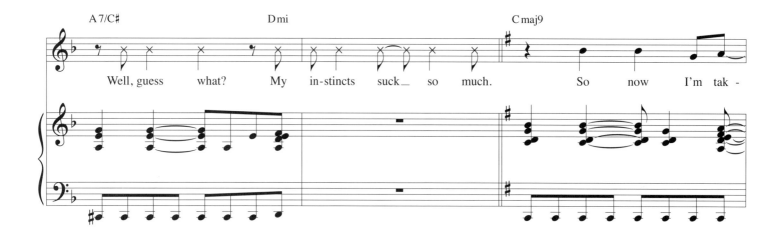

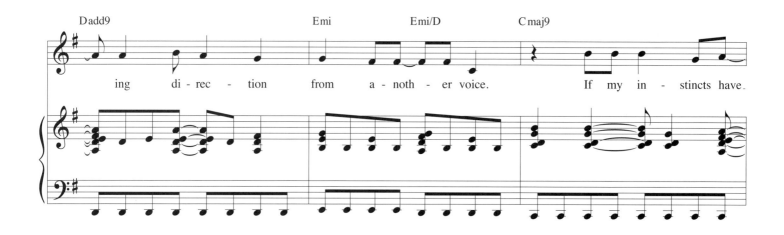

havÂing this way feels bizÂarre__ but if things keep up the way they are,__ then

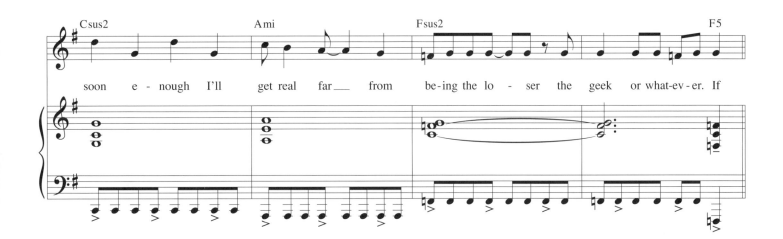

soon eÂnough I'll get real far__ from beÂing the loÂser the geek or whatÂevÂer. If

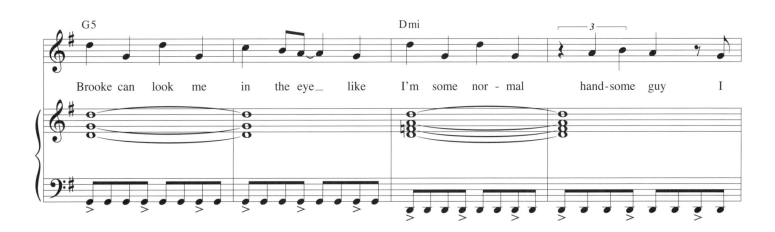

Brooke can look me in the eye__ like I'm some norÂmal handÂsome guy I

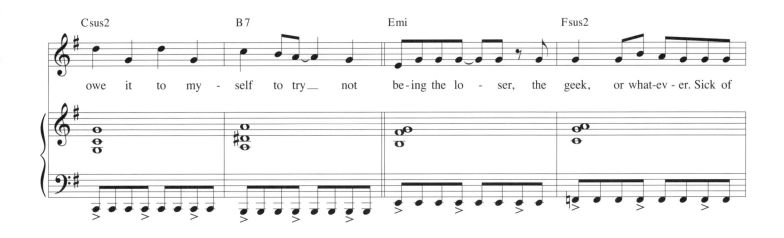

owe it to myÂself to try__ not beÂing the loÂser, the geek, or whatÂevÂer. Sick of

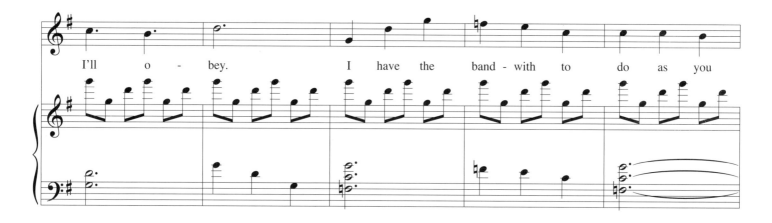

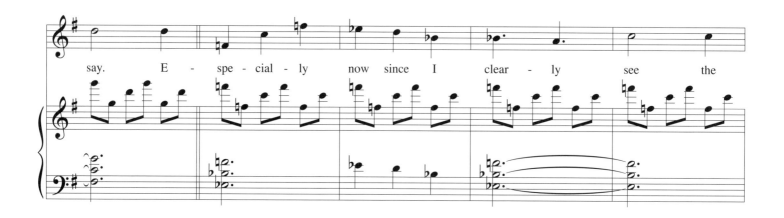

Slower - Colla Voce

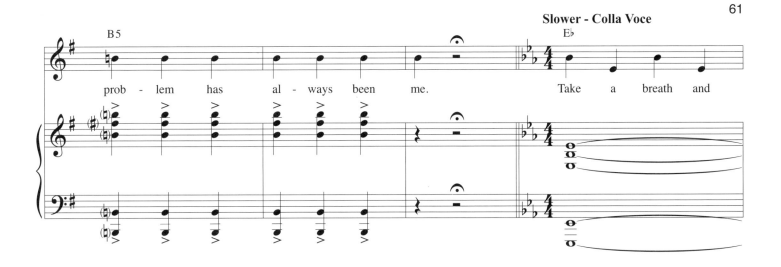

prob - lem has al - ways been me. Take a breath and

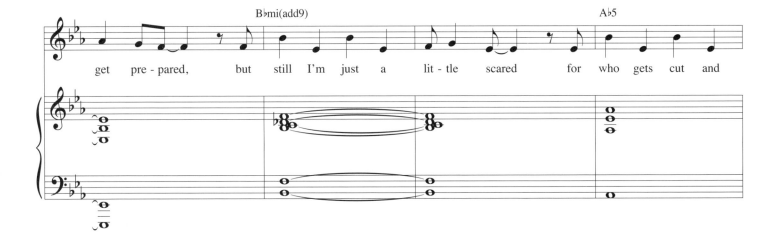

get pre - pared, but still I'm just a lit - tle scared for who gets cut and

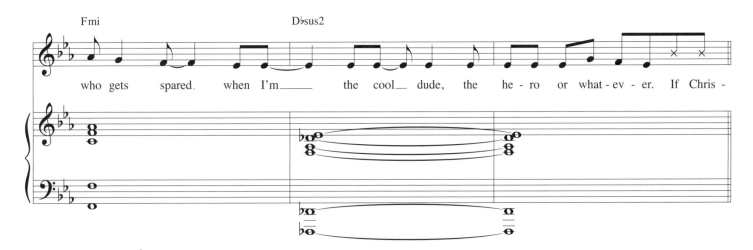

who gets spared. when I'm____ the cool__ dude, the he - ro or what - ev - er. If Chris -

A tempo, ♩ = 122

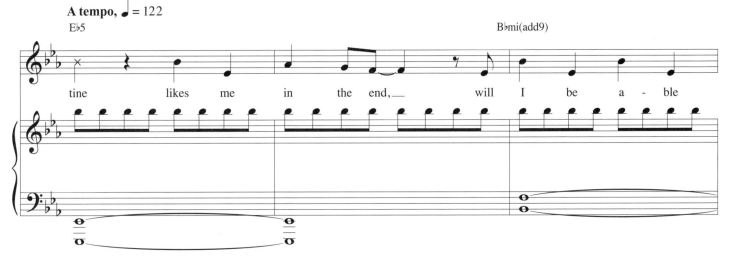

tine likes me in the end,____ will I be a - ble

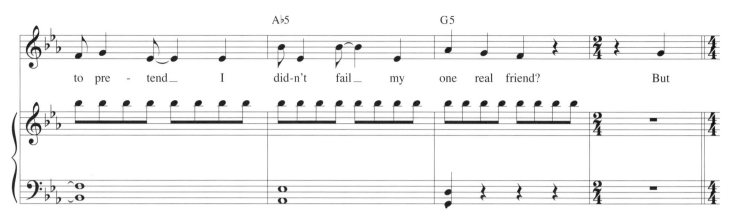

to pre-tend___ I did-n't fail___ my one real friend? But

A tempo, ♩ = 122

that's the shit___ I nor-mal-ly would think. Get o-ver it,___ get pri-or-

cresc. poco a poco

Accel. Poco a Poco

i-ties in sync. Just mute the voice___ in-side___ your head___ and con-

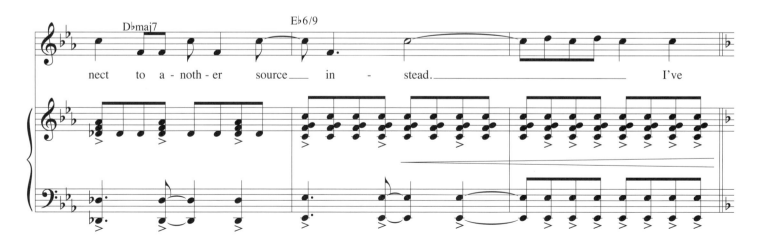

nect to a-noth-er source___ in-stead._____ I've

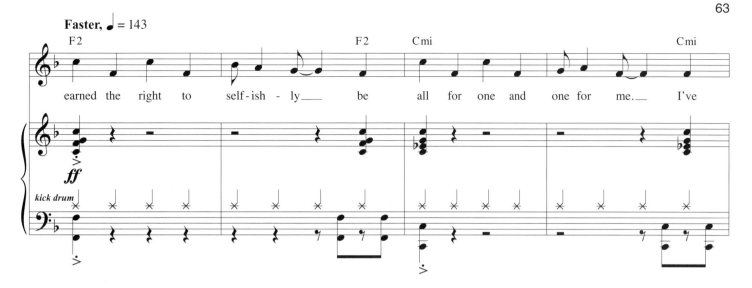

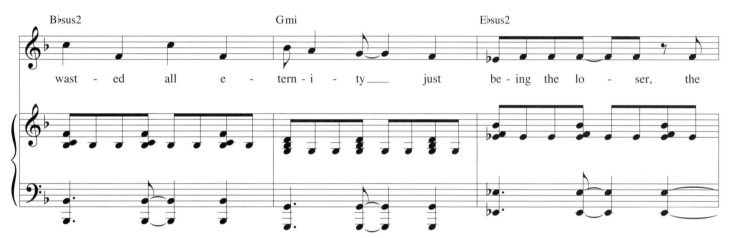

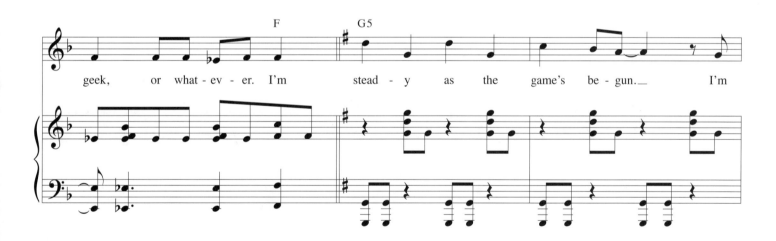

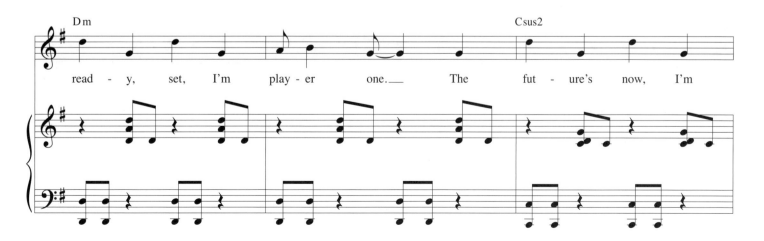

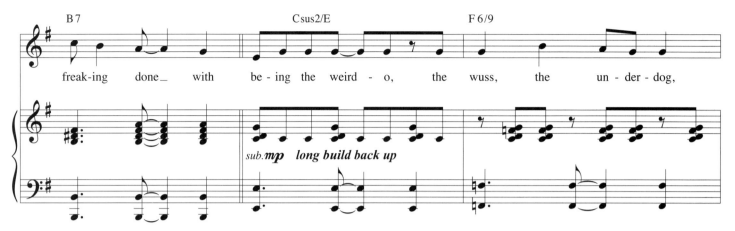

freak-ing done with be - ing the weird - o, the wuss, the un - der - dog,

sub. **mp** **long build back up**

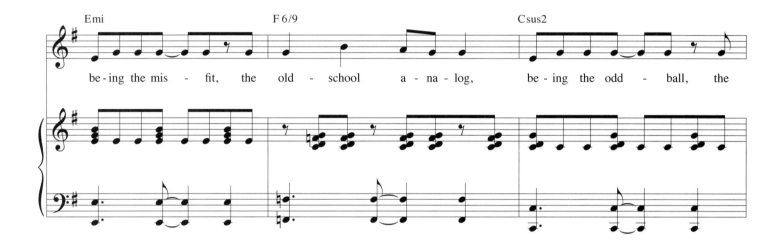

be - ing the mis - fit, the old - school a - na - log, be - ing the odd - ball, the

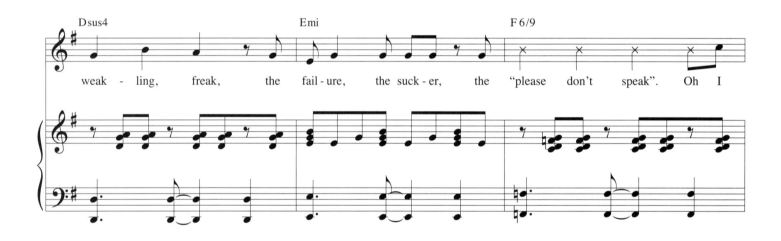

weak - ling, freak, the fail - ure, the suck - er, the "please don't speak". Oh I

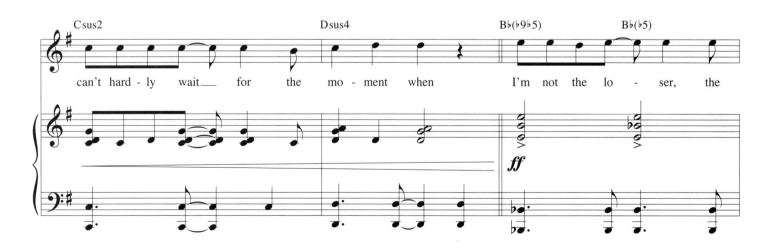

can't hard - ly wait for the mo - ment when I'm not the lo - ser, the

ff

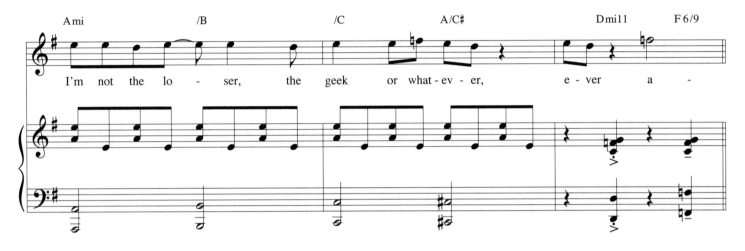

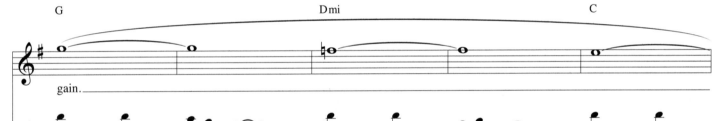

MICHAEL IN THE BATHROOM

from *Be More Chill*

Words and Music by
Joe Iconis

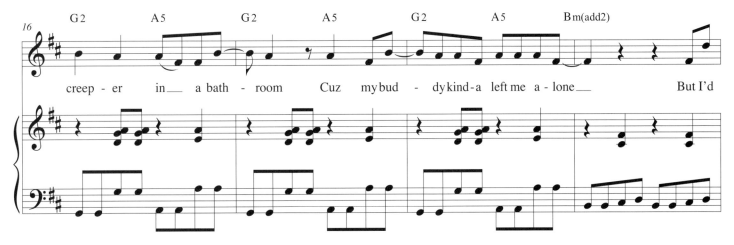

creep - er in__ a bath - room Cuz my bud - dy kind-a left me a - lone__ But I'd

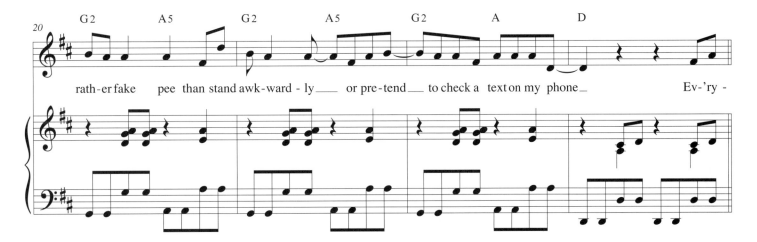

rath-er fake pee than stand awk-ward - ly__ or pre-tend__ to check a text on my phone__ Ev-'ry -

thing felt fine When I was half __ of a pair__ Now through no

fault __ of mine There's no oth - er half there_____ Now I'm just

Tempo I

self   All__ by him - self   I'm

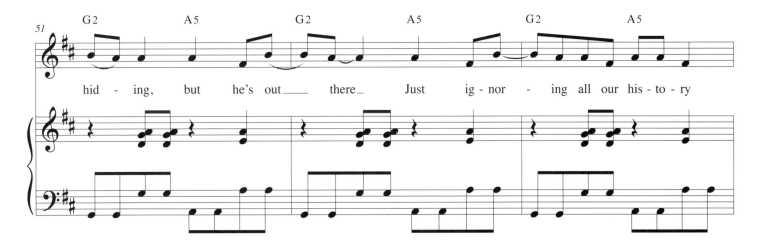

hid - ing, but he's out____ there__ Just ig - nor - ing all our his - to - ry

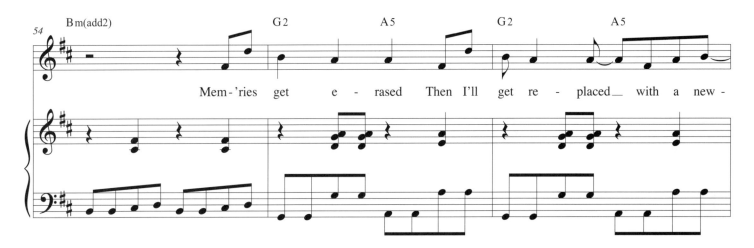

Mem - 'ries get e - rased Then I'll get re - placed__ with a new -

- er cool - er ver - sion of me_____ And I hear a drunk girl

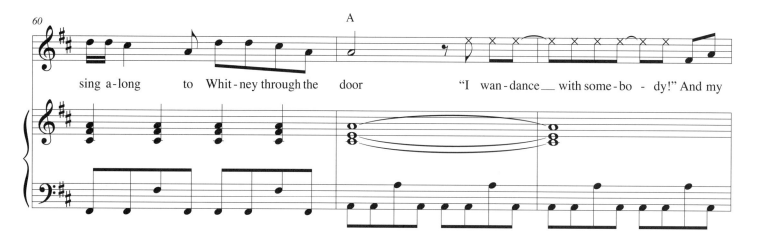

sing a-long to Whit-ney through the door "I wan-dance___ with some-bo - dy!" And my

feel - ings sink cuz it makes me think Now there's no_____ one to make fun of drunk girls

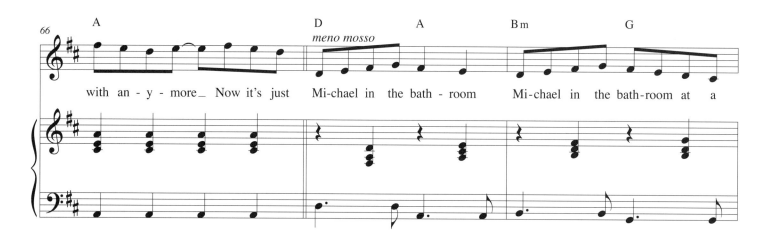

with an - y - more_ Now it's just Mi-chael in the bath - room Mi-chael in the bath-room at a

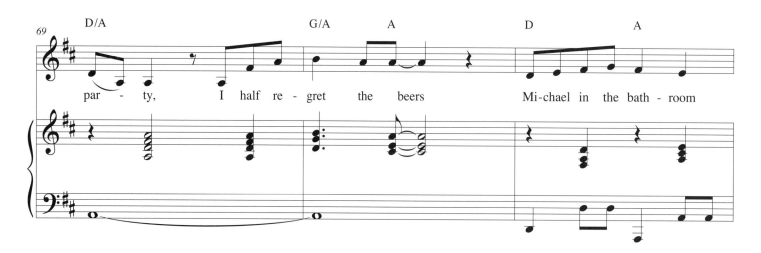

par - ty, I half re - gret the beers Mi-chael in the bath - room

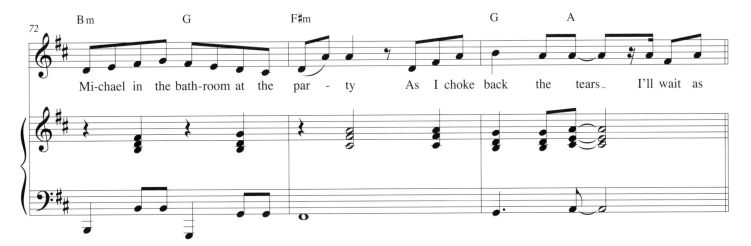

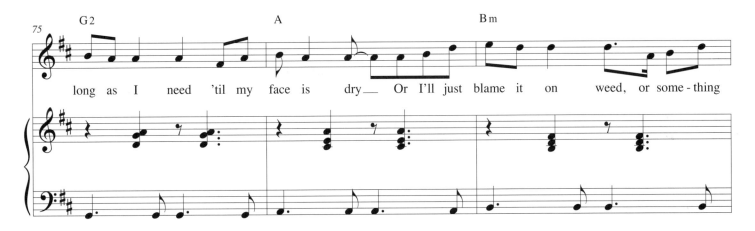

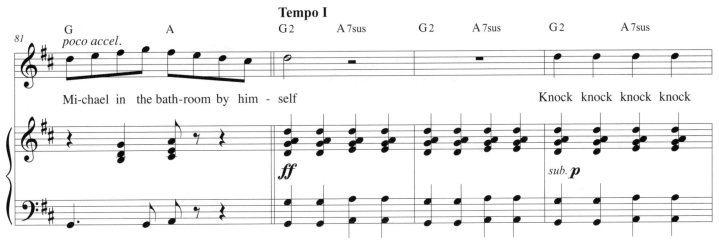

they're gon - na start to shout soon   Knock knock knock knock   aw hell yeah I'll be out __ soon

Knock knock knock knock   it sucks he left me here a-lone   Knock knock knock knock

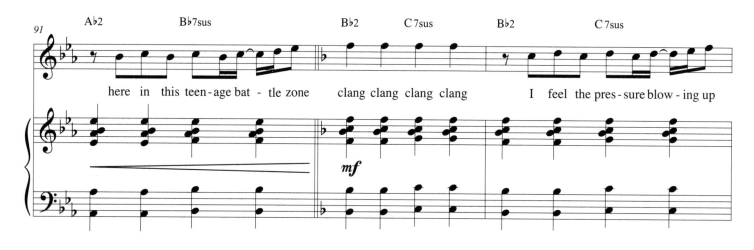

here in this teen-age bat - tle zone   clang clang clang clang   I feel the pres-sure blow-ing up

bang bang bang bang   my big mis-take was show-ing up   splash splash splash splash

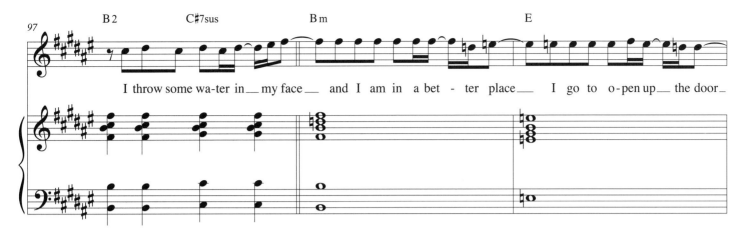

I throw some wa-ter in my face and I am in a bet - ter place I go to o-pen up the door

but can't hear knock-ing an - y-more

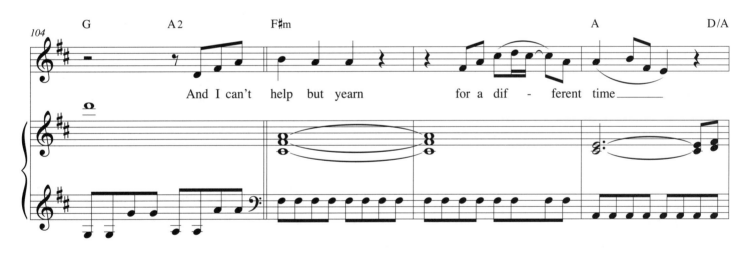

And I can't help but yearn for a dif – ferent time

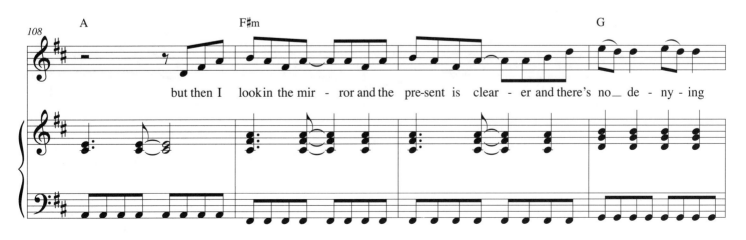

but then I look in the mir - ror and the pre-sent is clear - er and there's no de - ny - ing

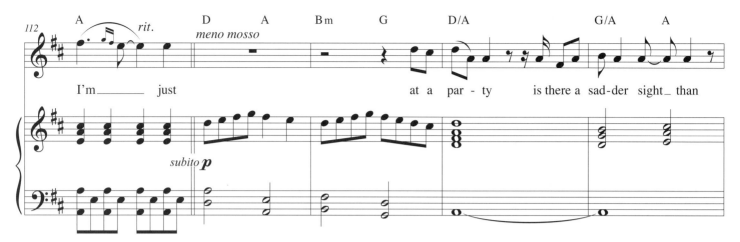

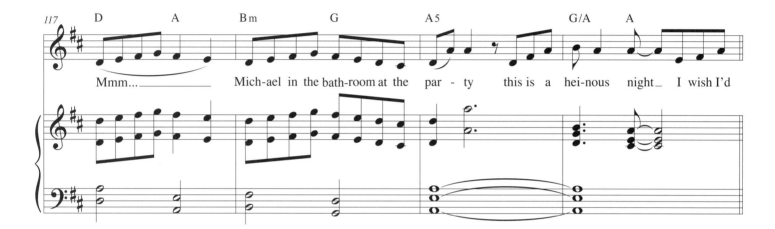

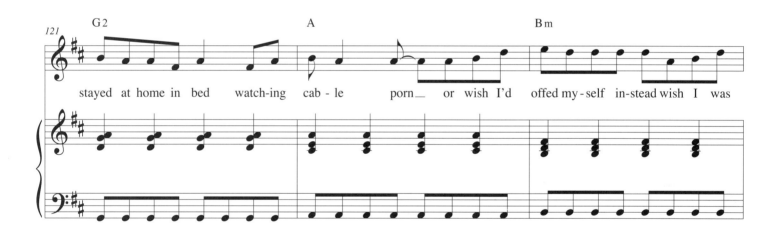

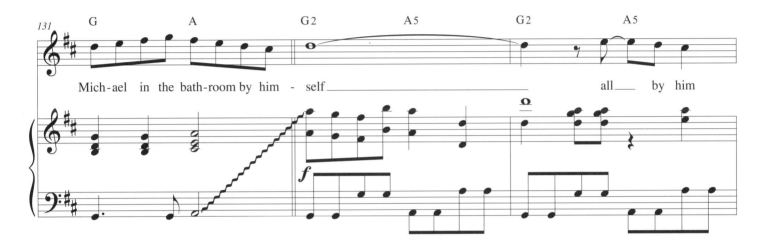

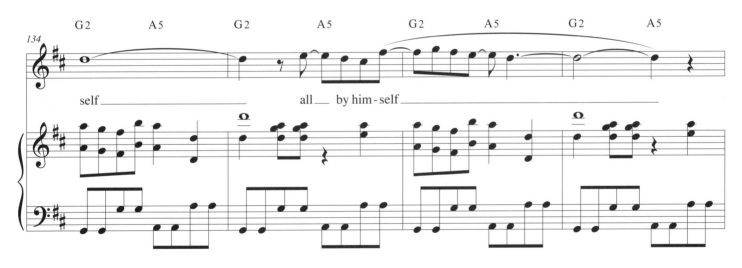

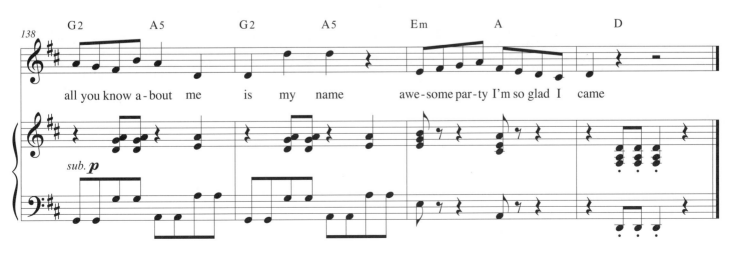

PROUD OF YOUR BOY
from *Aladdin*

Music by Alan Menken
Lyrics by Howard Ashman

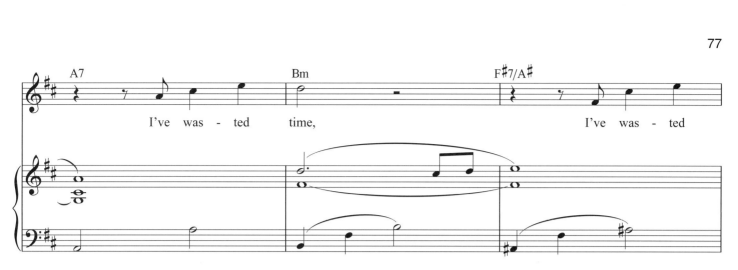

I've was - ted time, I've was - ted

me. So say I'm slow for my age, a late

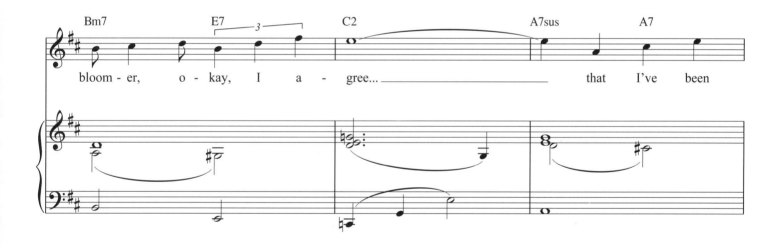

bloom - er, o - kay, I a - gree... that I've been

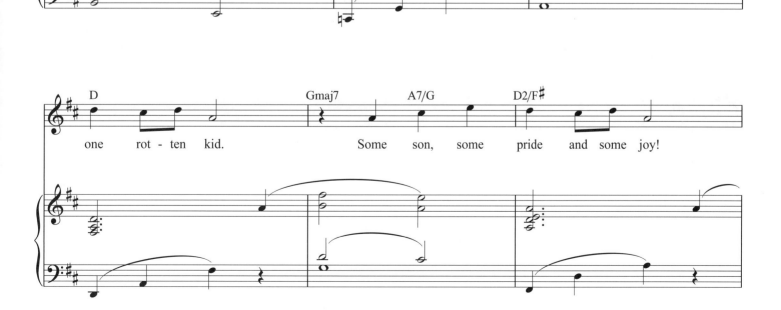

one rot - ten kid. Some son, some pride and some joy!

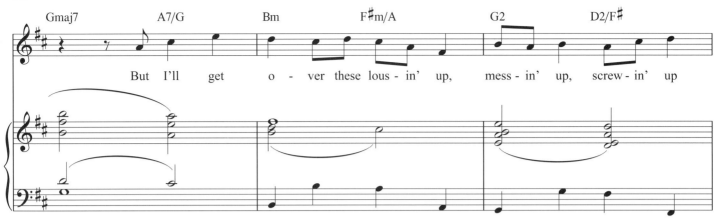

But I'll get o - ver these lous - in' up, mess - in' up, screw - in' up

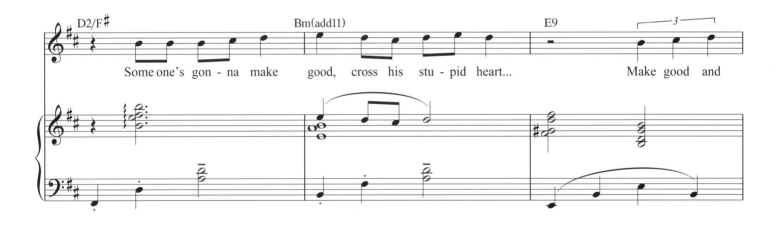

times. You'll see, Ma, now comes the bet - ter part.

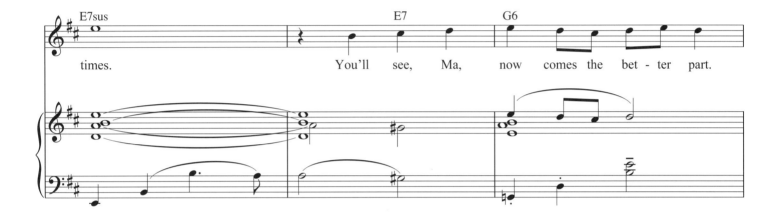

Some one's gon - na make good, cross his stu - pid heart... Make good and

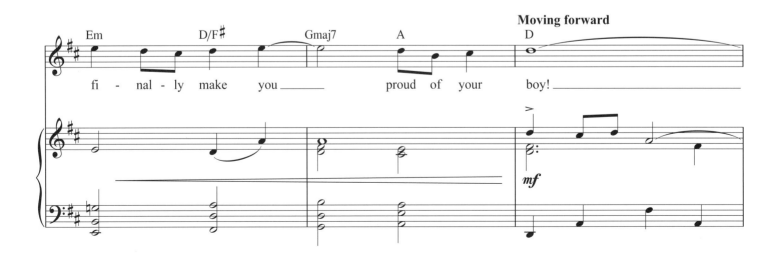

fi - nal - ly make you _____ proud of your boy! _____

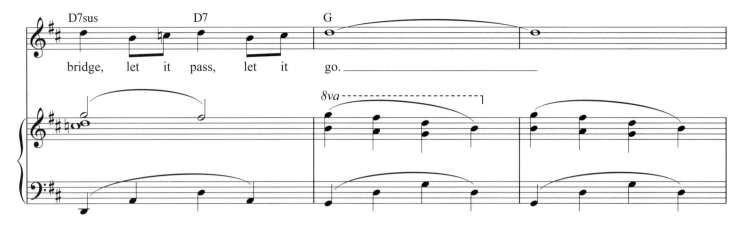

bridge, let it pass, let it go._____

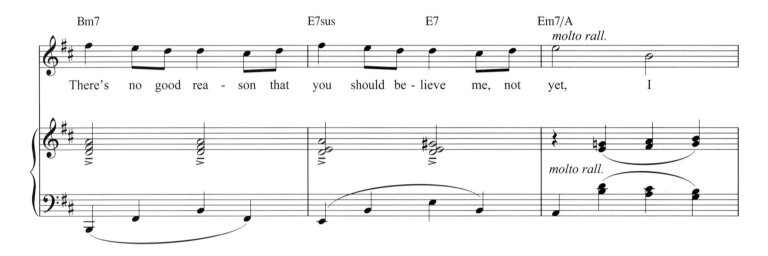

There's no good rea - son that you should be - lieve me, not yet, I

molto rall.

A tempo, grandly

know, but... Some - day and soon, I'll make you

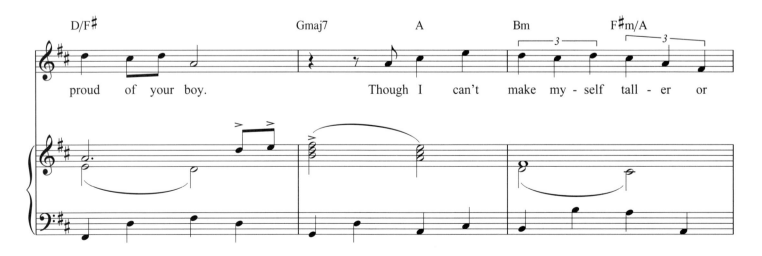

proud of your boy. Though I can't make my - self tall - er or

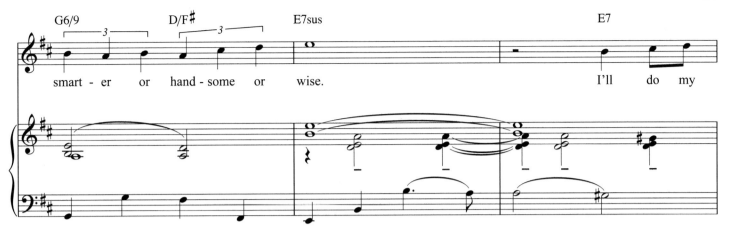

smart - er or hand - some or wise. I'll do my

best, what else can I do? Since I was - n't born per - fect like Dad or you

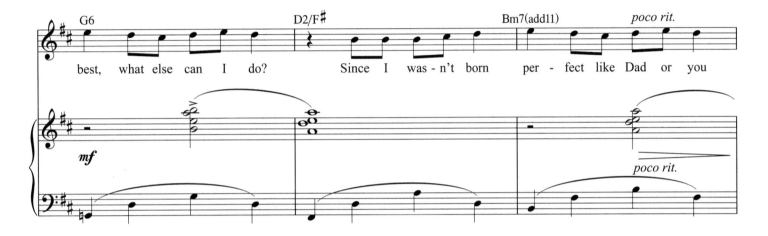

Mom, I will try to, try hard to make you proud of your

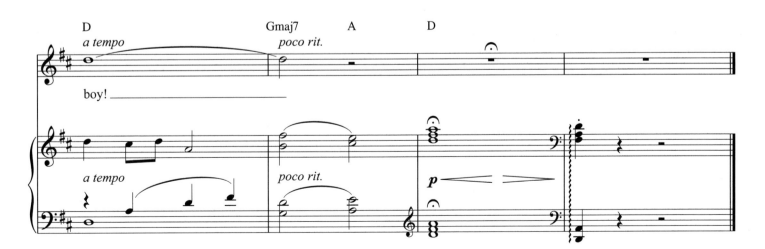

boy!

SANTA FE
from *Newsies The Musical*

Music by Alan Menken
Lyrics by Jack Feldman

fight - in', bleed - in', fall - in'. Thanks to good ol' Cap - tain Jack. Cap-tain

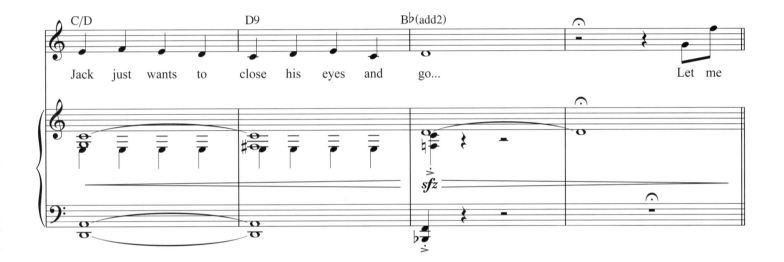

Jack just wants to close his eyes and go... Let me

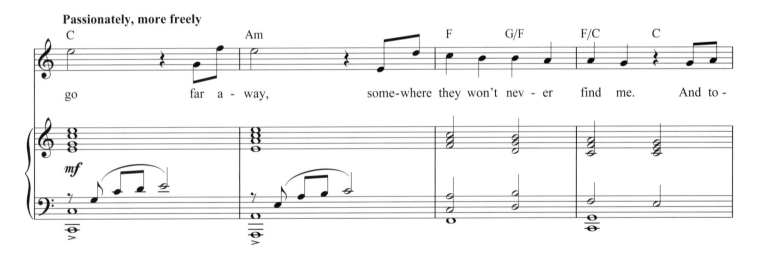

Passionately, more freely

go far a - way, some-where they won't nev - er find me. And to -

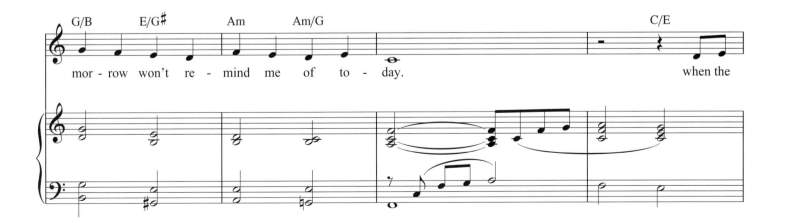

mor - row won't re - mind me of to - day. when the

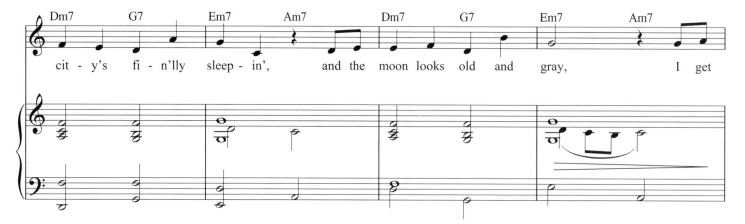

cit - y's fi - n'lly sleep - in', and the moon looks old and gray, I get

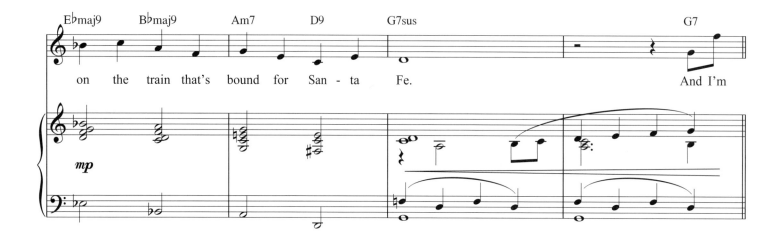

on the train that's bound for San - ta Fe. And I'm

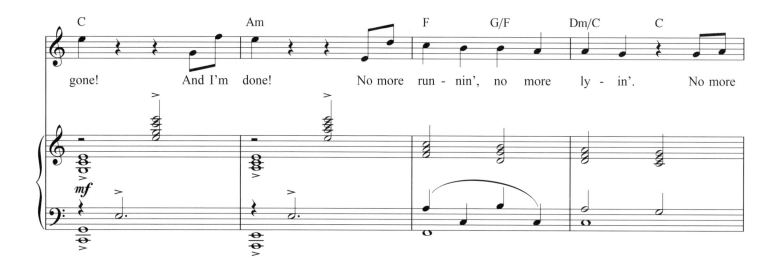

gone! And I'm done! No more run - nin', no more ly - in'. No more

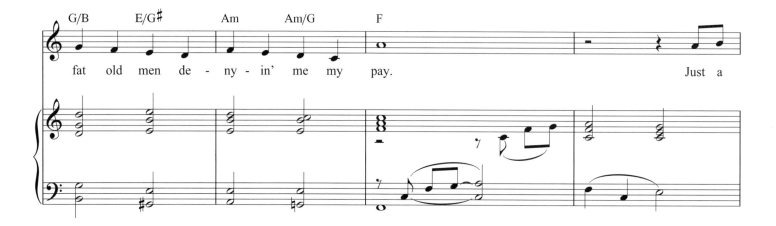

fat old men de - ny - in' me my pay. Just a

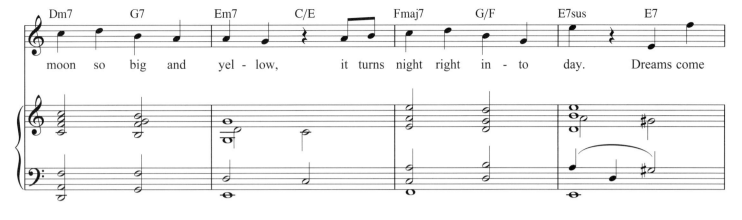

moon so big and yel-low, it turns night right in-to day. Dreams come

true, yeah, they do, in San-ta Fe.

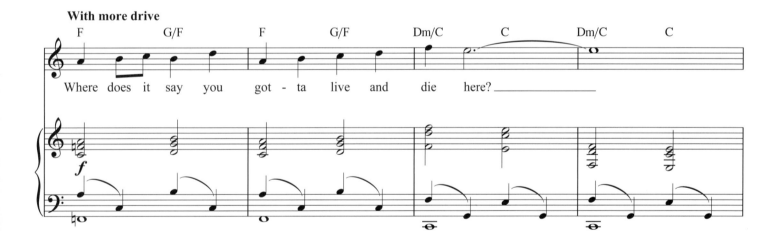

With more drive

Where does it say you got-ta live and die here?

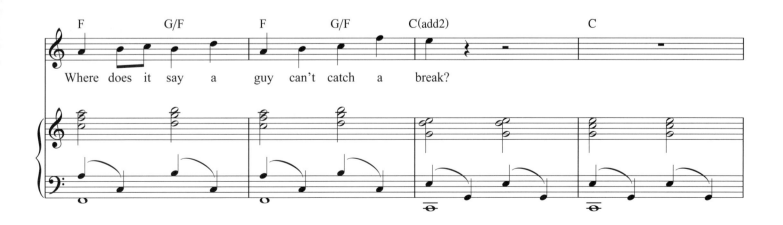

Where does it say a guy can't catch a break?

E7sus **Am(add2)** **Am(add2)/G** **G/A**

scene,   far from the lous - y   head - lines   and the   dead - lines   in   be -

molto rall.   **A7**   **Gmaj7/A**   **G/A**

tween! _____

A7sus **A7** **Broadly, in 4** **D** **Bm** **moving forward** **G** **A/G**

San - ta   Fe!   My old   friend!   I can't spend   my   whole   life

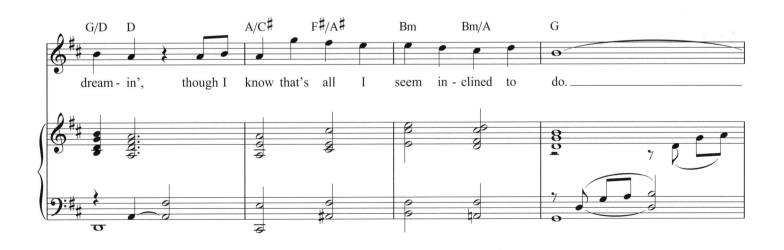

G/D **D** **A/C♯** **F♯/A♯** **Bm** **Bm/A** **G**

dream - in',   though I   know that's all   I   seem in - clined   to   do. _____

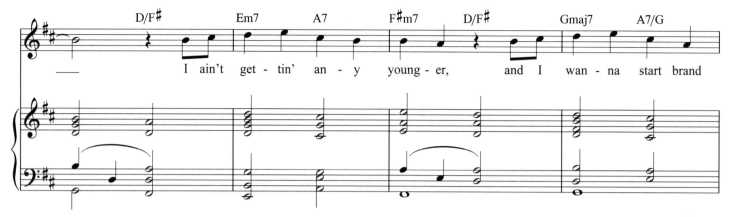

I ain't get-tin' an-y young-er, and I wan-na start brand

More Broadly

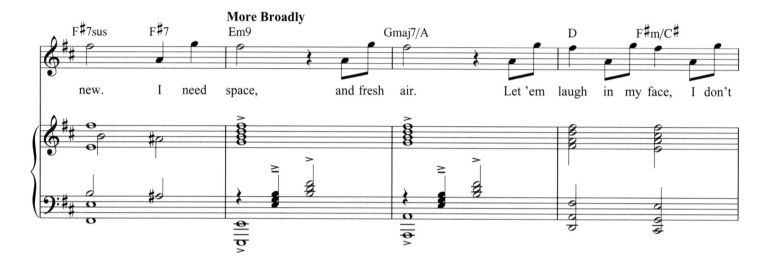

new. I need space, and fresh air. Let 'em laugh in my face, I don't

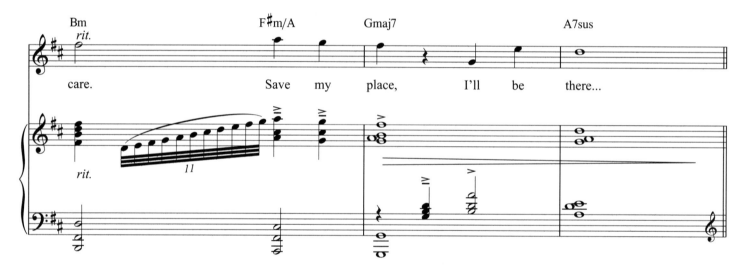

care. Save my place, I'll be there...

A tempo (poco rubato)

TOP OF THE WORLD
from *Tuck Everlasting*

Music by Chris Miller
Lyrics by Nathan Tysen

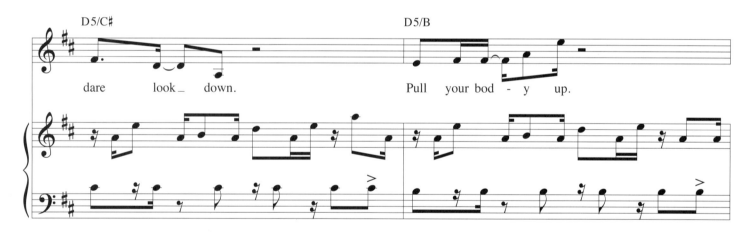

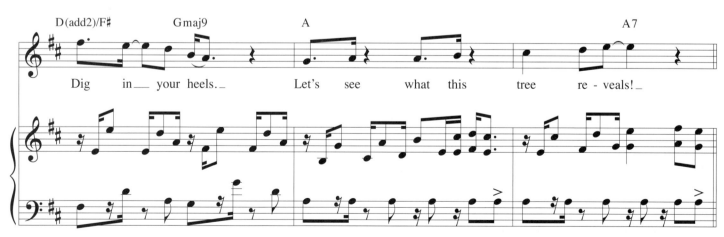

The song begins as a solo, and ensemble is added later. This edition has been adapted as a solo.

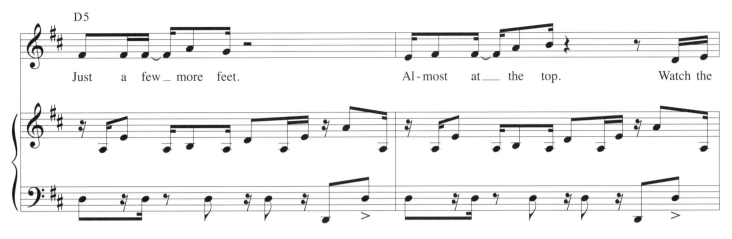

Just a few more feet. Al-most at the top. Watch the

rob - in's nest. Pull your bod - y up 'til

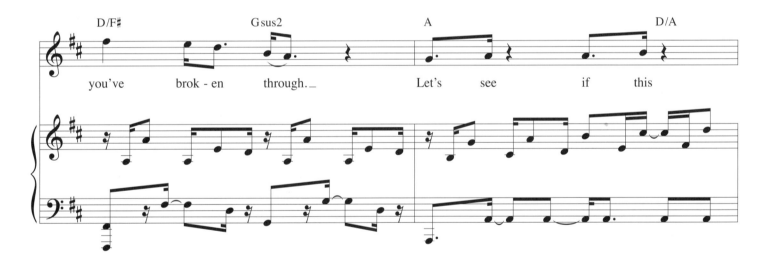

you've brok - en through. Let's see if this

tree has a view! At the top, at the top, at the top of the world you're

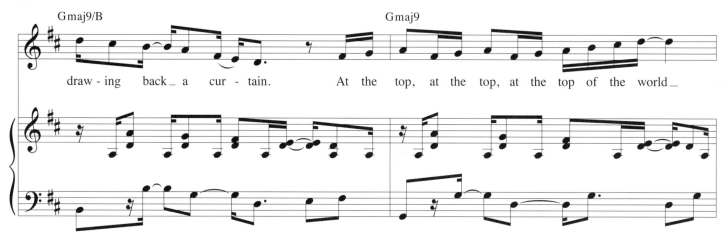

drawing back a curtain. At the top, at the top, at the top of the world

there you know for certain you're a-live, and

you are free. So fol-low me

to the top of the world.

Moun - tains to ___ the west. ___ An o - cean to ___ the east. ___ A

A/C♯   Bm7

storm - cloud to ___ the north   read - y ___ to pour. ___

D/F♯   Gsus2   A   D/A   A7

Ev - 'ry syc-a-more ___ leaves me ___ want - ing ___ more and more. ___ At the

Gmaj9   Gmaj9/B

top, at the top, at the top of the world ___ my head and heart ___ are pound - ing. At the

top, at the top, at the top of the world_ I hear my voice re-sound - ing:

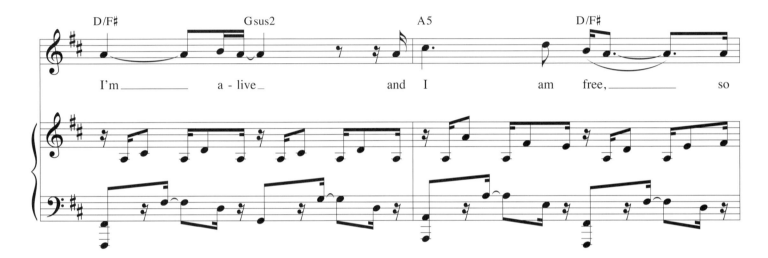

I'm_____ a - live_ and I am free,_____ so

look at_ me._____ I'll

go out on_ a limb._ Walk a tight - rope wire. For the

high - est height,_ yes, I'll risk_ it all._

Give me_ a bar-rel,_____ guess who'll_ find a___

wa - ter_ fall?__ At the top, at the top, at the top of the world_ my

head and heart_ are pound - ing. At the top, at the top, at the top of the world_ I

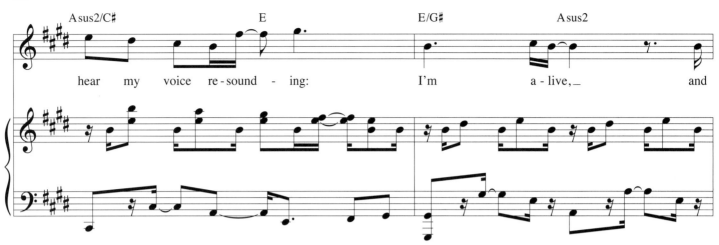

hear my voice re-sound - ing: I'm a-live,__ and

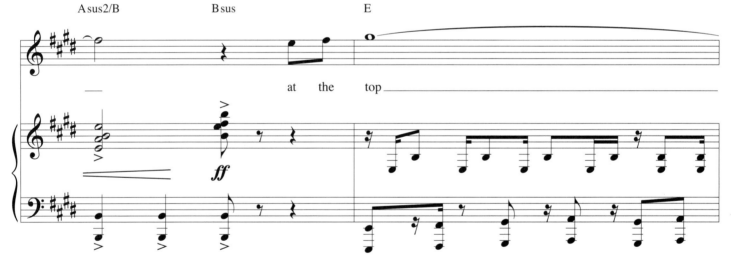

I am free.__ So look at__ me__

at the top__

of the world!__

WAVING THROUGH A WINDOW

from *Dear Evan Hansen*

Music and Lyrics by Benj Pasek
and Justin Paul

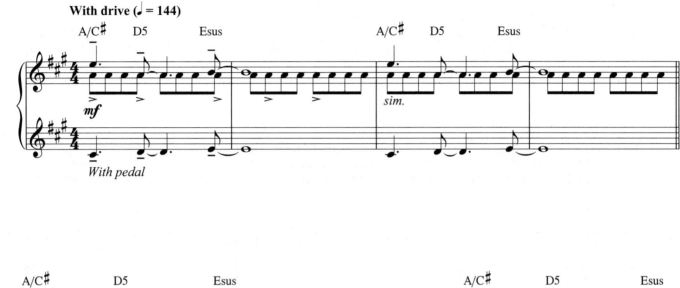

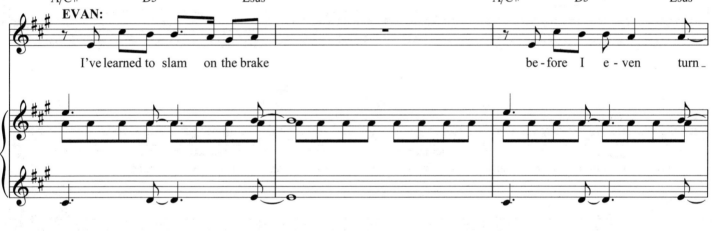

I've learned to slam on the brake before I even turn

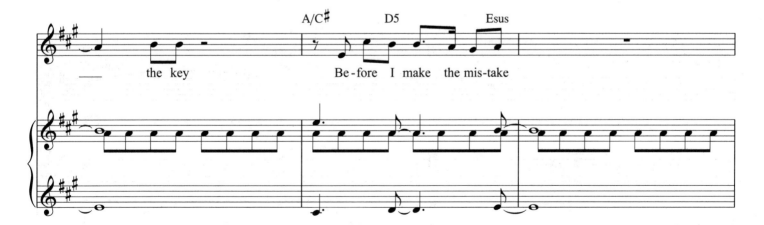

the key Be-fore I make the mis-take

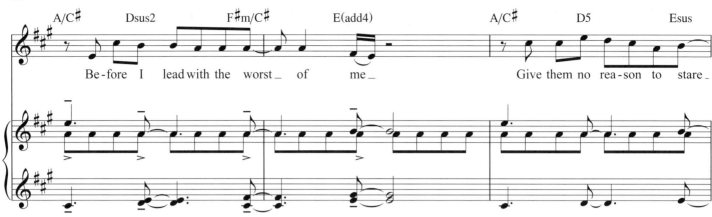

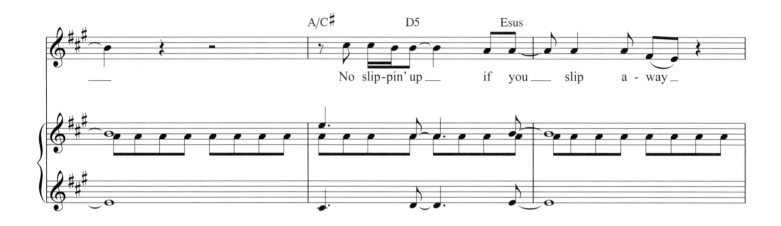

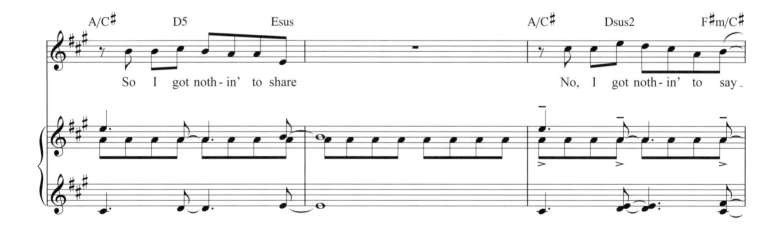

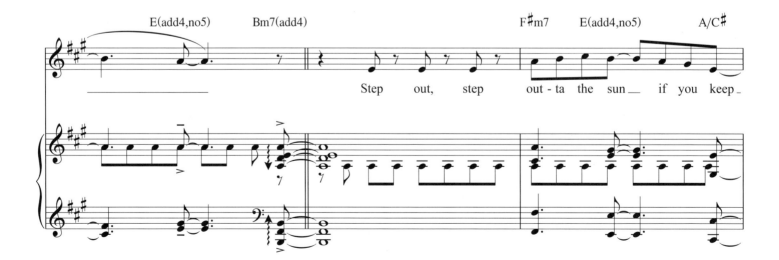

get - tin' burned ___   Step out, step

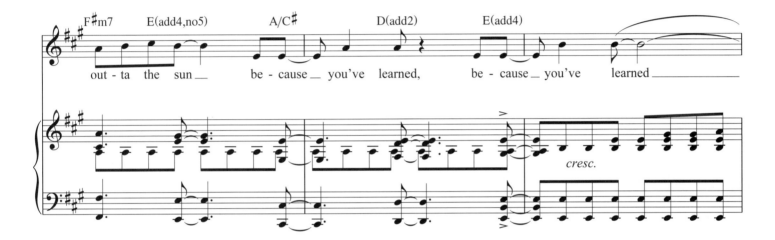

out - ta the sun ___ be - cause ___ you've learned, be - cause ___ you've learned ___

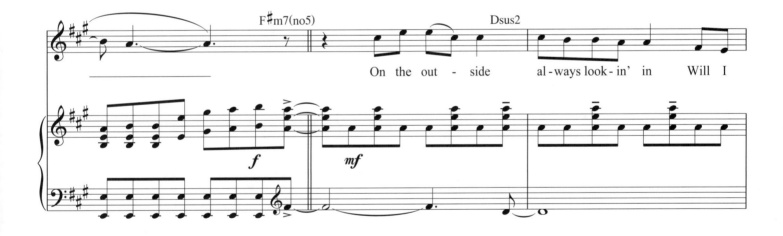

___ On the out - side al - ways look - in' in Will I

ev - er be ___ more than I've al - ways been? 'Cause I'm tap - tap - tap - pin' on the

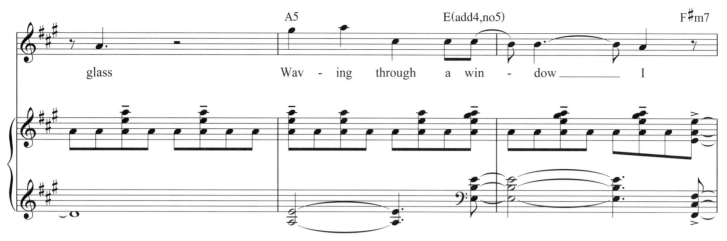

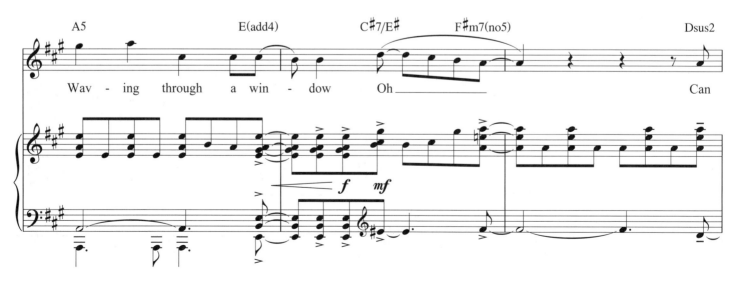

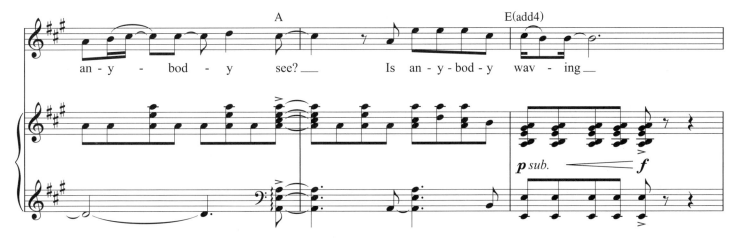

an-y - bod - y see?__ Is an-y-bod-y wav - ing__

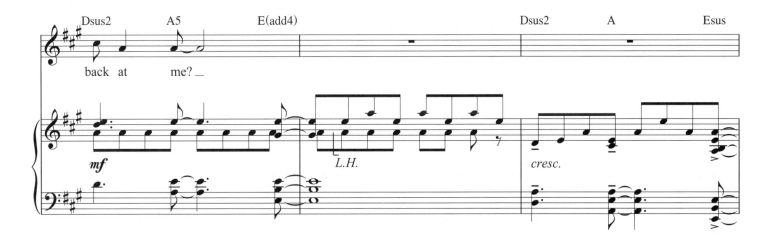

back at me? __

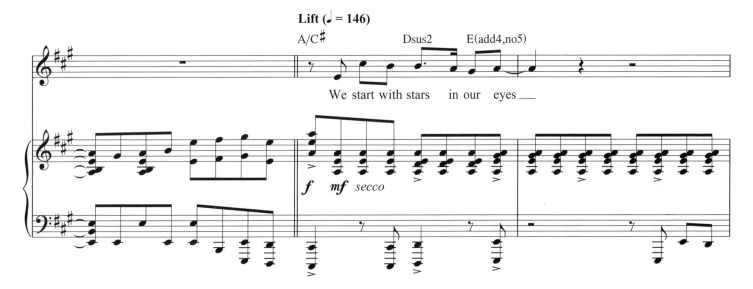

Lift (♩ = 146)

We start with stars in our eyes __

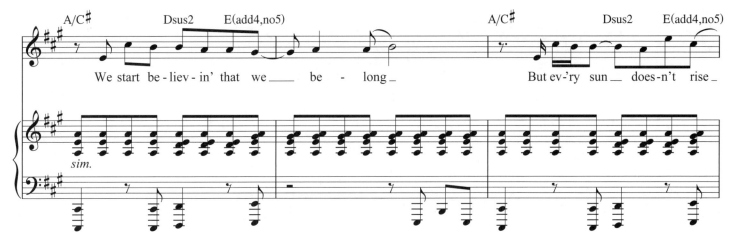

We start be-liev-in' that we __ be - long _ But ev-'ry sun _ does-n't rise _

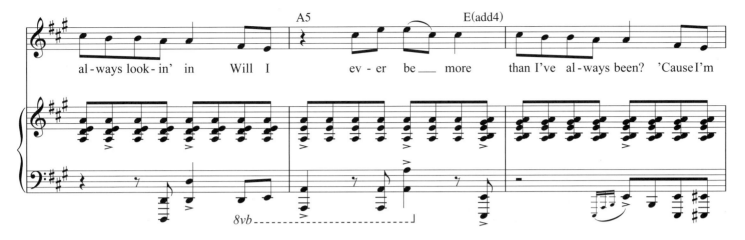

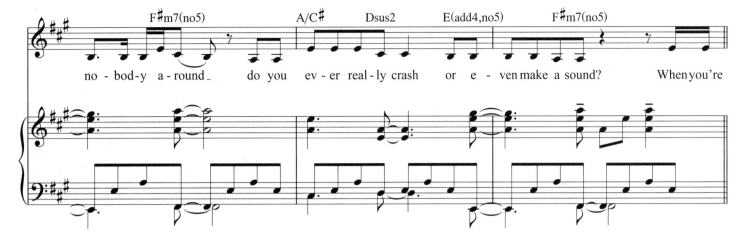

no-bod-y a-round__ do you ev-er real-ly crash or e-ven make a sound? When you're

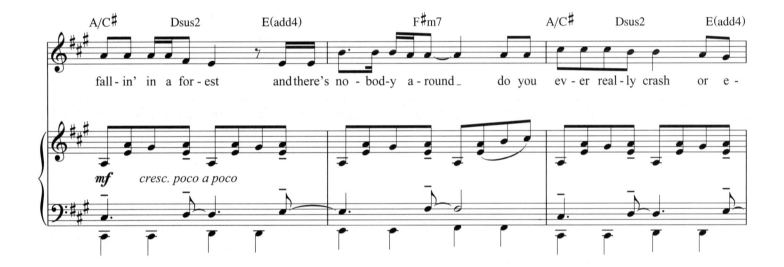

fall-in' in a for-est and there's no-bod-y a-round__ do you ev-er real-ly crash or e-

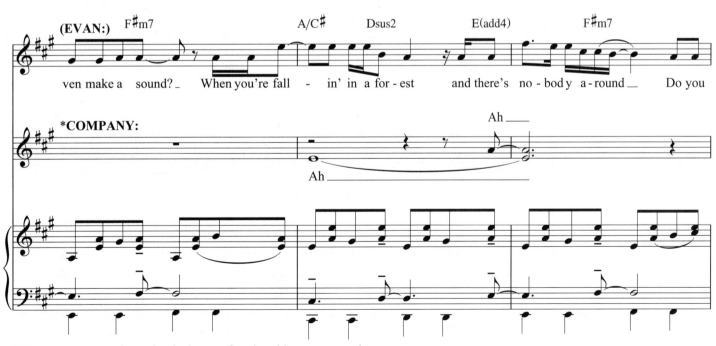

(EVAN:) ven make a sound?__ When you're fall-in' in a for-est and there's no-bod-y a-round__ Do you

*COMPANY: Ah____ / Ah____

*The company may be omitted when performing this song as a solo.

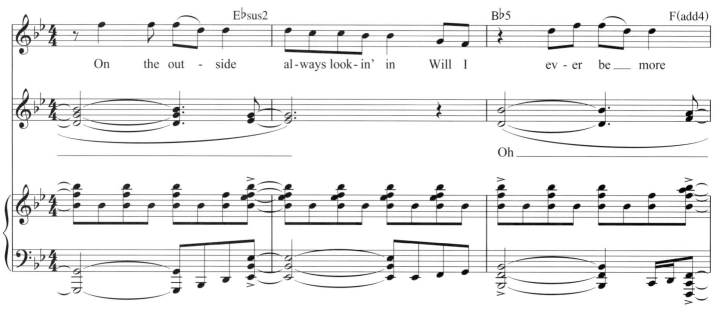

than I've al-ways been? 'Cause I'm tap - tap - tap-pin' on the ____ glass ____

Oh ____

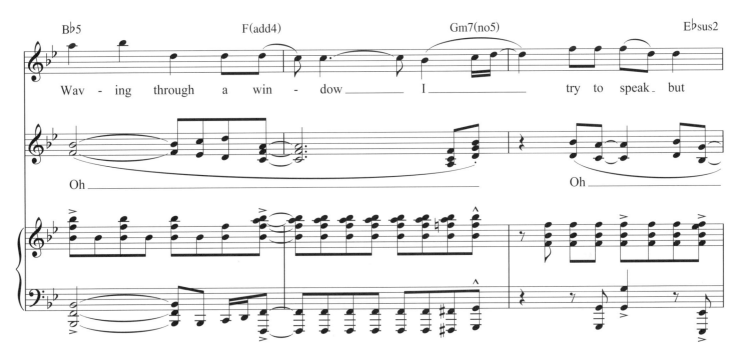

Wav - ing through a win - dow ____ I ____ try to speak ____ but

Oh ____ Oh ____

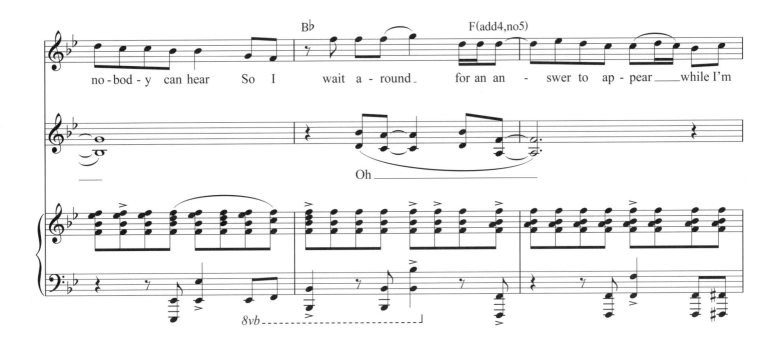

no-bod - y can hear So I wait a - round ____ for an an - swer to ap - pear ____ while I'm

Oh ____